CALIFORNIA DRIVERS TEST MADE EASY

Alice Syman

A former Driver Examiner

SYMAN PUBLISHING, ST. AUGUSTINE, FLORIDA

Our 32nd Year Helping California Drivers Pass Their DMV Tests

CALIFORNIA DRIVERS TEST MADE EASY

Alice Syman © 1981, 1983, 1984, 1987, 1998, 2001, 2005, 2008, 2010, 2013

Printed in the United States of America
ISBN: 0-941704-16-8 (pbk.)

WARNING-DISCLAIMER
This manual is designed to assist you in passing a California original or renewal Class C license test, and parts of other DMV tests. It is not guaranteed to include every question that may appear on DMV's tests, but rather to alert you to the type of questions which may appear thereon, and to acquaint you with the different ways they may be worded. Regulations are accurate up to the printing date and should remain current for several years. A copy of the latest *California DMV Driver Handbook* will alert you to any possible changes before this book is revised. The publisher/author shall have no liability or responsibility to any person with respect to any loss or damage caused or alleged to be caused by the information contained in this manual. If you do not wish to be bound by this disclaimer, you may return this book to the publisher for a full refund.

Syman Publishing
P.O. Box 5495
St. Augustine, FL 32085
904-810-5596
Email: asyman@earthlink.net

PRAISE FOR CALIFORNIA DRIVERS TEST MADE EASY

"California Drivers Test Made Easy will help you pass your test Big Time! " **—Kenny Morse, Mr. Traffic**, Los Angeles Award-Winning Radio and TV Talk Show Host, actor, and traffic school instructor. www.mrtraffic.com

"I breezed through my Class C test in no time; received a five-year license! I also used Alice's Motorcycle Test Book and passed easily. "**—B.H., Fallbrook, member, Motorcycle Racers Hall of Fame**

"I purchased this book for my teenage son to study for his driving permit. Great information... provides up to date law changes. The book was extremely helpful for him, but also taught me a number of things, even though I've been driving for over 30 years." **— S.S., Los Angeles**

"My wife and I believe this is the best book that has ever been written on the subject of driving." **—J.H., Los Angeles**

"I just wanted to thank you very much!!! I failed my first test... my husband bought your book... it helped me pass the written test today. Only missed one question... thank God for you doing this for people who really need help! THANK YOU!" **— S.K., Rowland Heights**

"I bought the first edition of your book quite a while ago and it helped me get a perfect score! Now 19 years later I find it the only real help available. Thanks again for a wonderfully helpful book! " **—M. P, PhD., Manhattan Beach**

"I am bringing my family to California for a 3-week vacation. I am studying the book so I don't run afoul of the law while we are there." **—P.S., Essex, UK**

"Your book was truly a help. Thanks for being there, in print and on the phone! " **—J.D., Los Angeles**

"I have every edition of your book, since 1981. I always make 100% on my test. Thank you for making our lives less stressful!" **—W.G. MD, San Diego**

"Fantastic! I made 100%. You really made my day! Thank you and God bless you!" **—R.V., Newbury Park**

"This is the best book I could find to help me write an article to help teenagers pass their drivers test." **—Sarah Bunting, *SEVENTEEN* MAGAZINE**

"I can't think of any suggestions for making your book better. It is fine the way it is." **—C.P., Novato**

"My wife and I have used your books since 1981. We always pass our tests. Thank you!" **—Col. R.S. (ret.) San Diego**

"I passed my test with a perfect score. Thanks for producing such a great study aid!" **—F.C., A.A.F. Chief Master Sgt. (ret.) Laguna Hills**

"This book will help me get my license back and I will be able to go back to work. Thank you!" **—E.B., Los Angeles**

"This book is a real confidence builder. I am glad I found it." **—Bob W., Lakeside**

"I would not have passed without the help of your book." **—M.J., Los Angeles**

"I would have paid any price for this book!" **—R.W., Los Angeles**

"Kudos to Alice for her novel idea. Thank you for your loyalty with updates!" **—C.K., Petaluma**

"100% after reading your great book two times!" I am buying copies for several friends." **—L.H., San Rafael**

I made 100% on my test for the first time!" **—A.S., Balboa**

ACKNOWLEDGMENTS

Thanks to all of you who helped make *CALIFORNIA DRIVERS TEST MADE EASY* the great study-aid that it is.

For many years, Leo Goulet of Dana Point, has monitored legislative actions affecting California drivers, and has alerted me to new laws I might have missed. He also scans driver help columns in the newspapers and sends me links to them. HONK, in the Orange County Register. www.honk@ocregister.com. is very helpful.

Leo, I can't thank you enough!

Thanks to my family: Wayne, Bob and Julie Hunt, and to my computer guru Bob McDonald, for coming to my rescue when computer problems threaten to push me over the edge.

To those whose kind words about the book continue to inspire me, and to those who offer suggestions to make it more helpful, *thank you!*

And as always, a special thank you to **California Department of Motor Vehicles** for their permission to use in this book, materials from their annual *CALIFORNIA DRIVER HANDBOOK*.

Happy, safe, driving. And wherever you go, go safely there and come safely home.

Alice Syman
P.O. Box 5495
St. Augustine, FL 32084
904-810-5596
Email: asyman@earthlink.net

TABLE OF CONTENTS

Signals for Drivers and Bicyclists
Visual Search/Looking Ahead

   Three- Second Following Rule.

   Seat Belts/Safety Belts
   Merging/Crossing/Exiting/Passing
   Don't Always Trust Other Driver's Signals
   Large Trucks and Buses
   School Buses
   Trolleys/Street Cars/Buses

   Motorcycles and Bicycles
   Train Crossings

   Financial Responsibility
   Drugs and Alcohol
   Pedestrians
   Roundabouts
   California Vision Exam requirements

ABOUT THE AUTHOR

ALICE SYMAN taught driver education10 years in her own professional driving school. She was a National Safety Council's Defensive Driving Course Instructor, and has worked as a driver examiner.

She wrote the first edition of *CALIFORNIA DRIVERS TEST MADE EASY* in 1981. Her extensive experience teaching driver education, and giving driver tests, made her very aware of the fear and apprehension experienced by most drivers when they have to take a DMV test. She wrote this book to try to help relieve those symptoms. The many thousands of copies sold, and the numerous calls, letters and emails she has received from those who have used it, proves that it does just that.

Alice lived in San Clemente, CA when she published the first edition of *CALIFORNIA DRIVERS TEST MADE EASY*. She now lives in St. Augustine, Florida.

WHO NEEDS THIS BOOK?

• **You** need it you are applying for an original Class C Driver License, a Class C License renewal, a Motorcycle License, an Adult Instructions Permit, or a Minor's Instruction Permit.

• **You** need it if you are 70 years of age or older and are applying for a renewal license.

• **You** need it if you have received two previous driver license renewal extensions.

• **You** need it if your license has been suspended or revoked and you are applying for reinstatement.

• **You** need it if you are a parent teaching your teen to drive.

• **You** need it if you teach high school driver education classes. It will shorten study time for students applying for an Instruction Permit. And it will sharpen your expertise as a classroom and behind-the-wheel driving instructor.

• **You** need it if you are visiting from another state or country and want to be sure you can drive safely and entirely within the law on California's complex roadway and highway systems

• **YOU** need it if you are beginning to feel less confident about your ability to drive a car safely, or if you just want to be sure you are up to date on all of DMV's traffic laws.

TRAFFIC LAWS PASSED IN RECENT YEARS
(And Some Older Laws)

§ MOTORCYCLE NOISE (2013)

Motorcycles manufactured after January 1, 2013, must be equipped with federally required emissions equipment.

§ HIGH OCCUPANCY TOLL LANE ACCESS (2013)

Single-occupant vehicles operated with natural gas or pure electric powertrains may travel in HOT lanes (High Occupancy Toll lanes) without paying the toll. For most HOT lanes the law takes effect January 1, 2013. For State Highways 10 and 110, the law will become effective March 1, 2014.

§ HANDS-FREE TEXTING (2013)

Drivers over 18 years of age may dictate, send or listen to a text message while driving, if their vehicle is specifically designed and configured to allow voice-controlled and hands-free operations.

Minor drivers may not send or read a text message when driving, even if the vehicle is equipped with a voice-controlled, hands-free device.

§ CHILD-PASSENGER RESTRAINTS (2012)

Children under the age of 8 years must ride in a federally approved child-passenger safety restraint system, unless they are 4 feet 9 inches tall and wear an appropriate safety belt.

§ ADMIN PER SE

When you drive in California, you consent to have your breath, blood or, under certain circumstances, urine tested if you are arrested for driving under the influence or alcohol, drugs, or a combination of both

MOVE OVER LAW   (2009)

§ Drivers are required to move over and slow down when approaching a roadside emergency along a state highway or freeway. The law is designed to reduce the deaths of police officers, tow truck drivers, paramedics and other emergency personnel who are aiding stranded or injured motorists.

§ IGNITION INTERLOCKING DEVICE (IID) (2009)

If you have a prior DUI conviction(s) and are convicted of driving with a suspended driver license, you will be required to install an Ignition Interlocking Device (IID) in your vehicle depending on your driving record.

An Ignition Interlocking Device (IID) works like a Breathalyzer. It measures your blood alcohol content (BAC). You breathe into it and, if your BAC is 0.01% or greater, your vehicle will not start.

Having a sober person blow in the IID to help you start the car may not work. Some IIDs are programmed to make you take the test again after you start driving.

SMOKING DRIVERS   (2008)

Smoking a cigarette, cigar or pipe when a person under age 18 is in the vehicle is illegal. The law applies whether or not the car is in motion.

§ ADULT DRIVERS AND CELL PHONES   (2008)

Adult drivers may **not** talk on a cell phone while driving unless it is equipped with a hands-free device.

Exception: An adult driver **may** use a cell phone to contact law enforcement or a public safety agency for emergency purposes.

§ MINOR DRIVERS AND CELL PHONES (2008)

Drivers under the age of 18 may **not** talk on a cell phone while driving, even if it is equipped with a hands-free device.

Exception: A driver under the age of 18 may use a cell phone to contact law enforcement or a public safety agency for emergency purposes.

§   If you are involved in an accident in which there was damage of $750, or there was an injury or a death, you must notify DMV within 10 days. For many years the reportable amount was "at least $500."

Remember: $750 ! (Not $500)

WHO MAY BE REQUIRED TO TAKE A BEHIND-THE-WHEEL DRIVING TEST?

- A person who has never been licensed in any state, or has a driver license from a foreign country

- Drivers with a vision-related problem

- A driver who has a limited term license for specified physical and mental (P&M) conditions

- Anyone requesting the removal of a DMV-imposed restriction for a physical condition (except corrective lenses)

- Anyone who has an out-of-state junior, provisional, or probationary license

- A driver who has been licensed out-of-state, but does not have a license to surrender

Behind-the-wheel driving tests for license renewals for holders of out-of-state or U.S. territory licenses are normally waived, if the license is presented. However, DMV may require a driving test at any time.

ALL DRIVING TESTS ARE THE SAME.

The driving test for the basic Class C license is the same for all drivers, regardless of age. An adult driver takes the same type of driving test as a teenage driver. **Exception: A driver with a physical and/or mental condition (P/M) may be required to take a different version of the driving test, which includes additional test elements.**

TEST DAY AT THE DMV

Be like the *smiling* folks in the DMV line above. The night before **TEST DAY** try to get a good night's sleep. Eat a good breakfast to get all your brain cells working. If possible, take your test early in the morning before you get brain-fade.

BE PREPARED. SAVE THE EXAMINER'S TIME.

Help the long lines at DMV move more quickly by having the DMV required documents in your hand when you reach the cashier. DMV's *CALIFORNIA DRIVERS HANDBOOK* will tell you what to bring: your old license, identification papers, driver education certificate, the license fee or whatever is required to obtain the license you are applying for.

DRIVER TEST ETIQUETTE

Some examiners "bark," but they're not allowed to bite. Facing long lines of desperate-to-pass people all day long can be, and usually is, very stressful. Keep that in mind as you work your way up the line. Be polite. Be courteous. Be patient.

SHH-H-H!

Don't talk to any other test takers as you are taking your test. Turn off all pagers and cell phones.

NO CHEATING!

Don't take this book, cheat sheets, or any other test aid into the testing area. If you are caught cheating, your test will be marked as a "failure" and DMV may take action against your driving privilege.

IS IT LEGAL TO USE THIS BOOK TO PREPARE FOR A DRIVER TEST?

Yes! This book is not a "cheat sheet." Its questions and answers are based on statements and assertions in DMV's Driver Handbook, and are used with DMV's permission. It pinpoints the rules and regulations you must know to pass your test, but you must also be familiar with the entire contents of DMV's free *CALIFORNIA DRIVER HANDBOOK* in order to drive entirely within the law. As you take the tests in this book, refer to that manual for a more detailed explanation of its questions and answers.

GOOD DRIVERS MAY BE BAD TEST TAKERS.

You may have heard these famous last words: "Been driving 50 years. Never had an accident. Never got a ticket. What's to be afraid of on a little ole driving test? If you're a good driver the test will be a snap!"

That driver may be in for a big let-down. He may not recognize in the test questions the rules and regulations he follows that makes him the good driver he is.

Your test may give your brain cells a real workout, but if you study this book very carefully it will be much easier, and you will make a high score—if not 100%. And remember, you must study California DMV's *CALIFORNIA DRIVER HANDBOOK* along with this book..

TEST-TAKING STRATEGY, Ed Newman, Ph.D.

REDUCE TENSION

Before the test, focus on your breathing. When you begin to feel anxious before or during the test, **breathe in...(deeply), breathe out..., breathe in...(deeply), breathe out....** Deep breaths not only reduce tension, they pump more oxygen to the brain and help you think more clearly.

TEST-TAKING STRATEGY

1) Read through the test and mark the <u>easiest</u> answers first.

2) Read the test a second time and answer the <u>more difficult</u> questions.

3) Go over the test a third time. Make sure all questions are answered, even if you are not sure of the answers. You may score enough correct answers to make a passing grade, or even 100%.

Give yourself time to master the tests. Don't wait until the last minute and have to cram. If you don't pass the first time, review the practice tests in this book, read DMV's *CALIFORNIA DRIVER HANDBOOK* and take the test again in a few days. The longer you wait the harder it is to go back.

THE WRITTEN TEST

California DMV tests are multiple-choice tests and can be quite wordy. One test question writer said he spends about 30 minutes composing each test question. Is it any wonder that it may take us about that long to decide how to answer a question, and still miss it?

Most DMV tests have several questions that are answered with numbers (days, speed limits, distances etc.). 5 days, 10 days. 15mph, 25mph, 55mph, 65mph, 70mph. 7 ½ feet, 15 feet, 100 feet, 200 feet, 300 feet, 500 feet. 0.01%, 0.08%. 3 seconds, 5 seconds, 10 to 15 seconds. $500, $750, $1000. Try to remember the numbers.

Some drivers say there was a question or two on their written test that had no answer in DMV's Driver Handbook. Read the DMV book again. It was there. You just overlooked it.

Then, there are some older drivers (younger drivers, too) who feel that DMV makes the tests difficult to try to get them off the road. Not so.

There are a number of licensed drivers in California who are over 100 years old. A Goleta, CA woman, 105 years old, recently passed a driver test with a good score. DMV only wants to keep unsafe drivers off the road; unsafe older drivers, as well as unsafe younger drivers.

And putting this as gently as I know how: if you should fail, don't alibi that you were just too nervous. Nervousness is rarely the cause. You fail because you are not prepared. You didn't study enough.

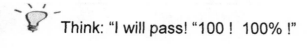 Think: "I will pass! "100 ! 100% !"

9

PRACTICE TEST No. 1

SOME NEW (and some old) TEST QUESTIONS

1. It is illegal for <u>anyone</u> to smoke in a car:
☐ Unless the windows are open
☐ Unless they are sitting in the back seat
☐ When there is a **minor** in the car

Answer: _____

2. Drivers under 18 years of age:
☐ May talk on a cell phone while driving
☐ May **not** talk on a cell phone while driving
☐ May talk on a cell phone with a hand-held device

Answer:_____

3. Single occupancy vehicles are exempt from paying tolls when driving in a High Occupancy Toll lane (HOT lane) if they:
☐ Don't drive any faster than 55 mph
☐ Drive the maximum speed limit
☐ Are operated with natural gas or pure electric powertrains

Answer:_____

4. California drivers <u>over</u> 18 may dictate, send or listen to a text message when driving if:

☐ The vehicle is equipped with a hands-free voice -operated equipment
☐ They use a cell phone
☐ A person 25 years old is in the vehicle

Answer:_____

5. Adult drivers may use a cell phone when driving if:

☐ They need to cancel an appointment
☐ The vehicle is equipped with a hands-free device
☐ They are late for work

Answer: _____

6. Motorcycles manufactured after Jan. 1, 2013 must:

☐ Not carry a passenger
☐ Be equipped with federally required emissions equipment
☐ Travel in the left lane

Answer:_____

7. Children under 8 years of age, or less than 4 feet 9 inches tall, must:

☐ Ride in federally approved safety restraint system
☐ Wear a regular seat belt
☐ Ride in the front seat of a vehicle

Answer:_____

8. You must notify law enforcement, and file with DMV a Traffic Accident Report (SR-21) if you:
☐ Have a flat tire on the freeway
☐ Are in a collision in which there was an injury or a death
☐ Hit a tree on the side of the road

Answer: _____

9. A minor may not use a cell phone when driving:
☐ Unless an adult is in the vehicle
☐ Unless the vehicle is equipped with hands-free equipment
☐ Except to contact law enforcement in an emergency

Answer: _____

10. If you are involved in an accident in which the damage is $_____or more, or someone was killed or injured you must make a written report to DMV within 10 days.
☐ $100
☐ $500
☐ $750

Answer: _____

11. If you abandon or dump an animal on a roadway:
☐ You may be fined up to $1000
☐ You won't be fined, if it is on a leash
☐ It will find a good home

Answer:_____

Remember: $750 (Not $500)

12. If you see an injured animal on a public roadway:

☐ Call 911 or CHP (California Highway Patrol)
☐ Leave it there. Animal Control will pick it up
☐ Leave it there. It will find a good home

Answer:_____

13. If you sell or transfer your vehicle to another person, you must report it to DMV:

☐ Within 5 days
☐ Within 10 days
☐ Within 30 days

Answer:_____

14. If you violate a restriction on your license:

☐ DMV may suspend your license
☐ DMV will make you take a driving test the same day
☐ DMV will cancel your insurance

Answer:_____

15. Drivers <u>over</u> 21 who drive with a blood alcohol content (BAC) of 0.08 %:

☐ Are driving legally
☐ Are driving illegally
☐ May drive on country roads only

Answer:_____

💡 **Think: "Drivers <u>over</u> 21—0.08%"**

16. DMV will not issue a license to a person whose best-corrected vision is:

□ 20/20

□ 20/40

□ 20/200 or worse

Answer:_____

17. A passenger vehicle may not tow:

□ More than one vehicle

□ A house car (RV)

□ Another passenger vehicle

Answer:_____

18. It is illegal to leave a child six years of age or under in a car unless the child:

□ Is attended by a person 12 years of age or older

□ Is asleep

□ Can unlock the doors

Answer:_____

19. Drivers involved in accidents must exchange driver license information and:

□ Proof of insurance

□ Proof of insurance and vehicle registration

□ Proof of insurance, vehicle registration, and address

Answer:_____

20. You are on probation for a driving violation. You refuse to take an alcohol screening (PAS) test or a chemical test:
□ Your driving privilege will be revoked for 2 years
□ Your driving privilege will be suspended
□ DMV will impound your vehicle

Answer:_____

21. Attempting to evade (run from) a police officer is punishable by:
□ One year in county jail
□ One year in state prison
□ A $5,000 fine

Answer:_____

22. If you let an unlicensed or suspended person drive your car:
□ It may be impounded (taken away) for 30 days
□ Your insurance will cover the driver
□ Your license will be canceled

Answer:_____

23. You are crossing a divided highway. There is a second stop sign on the divider strip. You should:
□ Stop at the first stop sign only
□ Stop at the second sign only if cars are coming
□ Stop again at the second stop sign

Answer: _____

24. Always STOP your vehicle at these traffic signals:
□ Solid red lights, flashing red lights and green lights
□ Solid red lights, flashing red lights and green arrows
□ Solid red lights. Flashing red lights. Blacked-out traffic signals.

Answer: _____

25. What is the difference between red arrows and solid red lights is?

□ You **cannot** turn against a red arrow, even if you stop first
□ Red arrows only stop traffic which is turning left
□ Red are arrows used for protected left turns

Answer: _____

26. No signal lights are working. You should:
□ Do as if the intersection were controlled by stop signs
□ Yield to all other vehicles
□ Drive through the intersection without stopping

Answer: _____

27. A signal light is flashing red. Stop, then:
□ Proceed (go ahead) when it is **safe** to do so
□ Go ahead without checking traffic
□ Drive slowly through the intersection

Answer: _____

28. A sign like this at an intersection means:

□ You may not make a Right Turn

□ You may not make a Left Turn

□ You may not make a U-TURN

Answer: _____

29. This sign warns that there is a:

□ Pedestrian crossing ahead

□ School crossing ahead

□ Construction flagman ahead

Answer: _____

30. This 3-sided red and white sign means you must:

□ Give right of way to other drivers

□ Stop before you cross the intersection

□ Not enter this street

Answer: _____

31. Where would you see this sign?

□ Near a school

□ In front of a church

□ At a pedestrian crosswalk

Answer:_____

32. This sign tells you:

- ❏ You may stop in the area for a while
- ❏ There is a hospital ahead
- ❏ All traffic must turn right

Answer: _____

33. When you see this sign you must:

- ❏ Slow down. Look for trains. Be prepared to stop
- ❏ Look for cars crossing the intersection
- ❏ Stop at the railroad tracks

Answer: _____

34. This sign means you must:

- ❏ **Stop**, check traffic in all directions, then go ahead
- ❏ **Slow down,** then go ahead
- ❏ **Stop**, then drive slowly through the intersection

Answer: _____

35. This sign means:

- ❏ There is a roundabout ahead
- ❏ You must turn left
- ❏ You may not make a U-TURN

Answer: _____

36. Children less than 4 feet 9 inches tall must:

- ❏ Be secured in a federally-approved safety restraint system
- ❏ Not ride bicycles in a public park
- ❏ Ride in the front seat of a vehicle

Answer _____

Read the True Statements below. Check your answers on page 22.

Statements marked with an arrow (▶) may be the answer to a question on your test. Study it carefully.

TRUE STATEMENTS

▶An adult may <u>not</u> use a cell phone while driving unless it is equipped with a hands-free device.

▶Minors may NOT talk on a cell phone while driving except to report an emergency.

▶No one may smoke in a car with a minor passenger.

▶If you see an emergency vehicle on the freeway with flashing lights, you must reduce your speed or move to another lane (New law 2007).

▶Minors may <u>not</u> send or read a text message while driving.

▶ If you are on probation for a DUI offense and operate a motor vehicle with a BAC of 0.01%, your driving privilege will be suspended for one year.

▶Refusing or failing to complete a preliminary alcohol screening (PAS) test or a chemical test will cause your driving privilege to be revoked for 2 years.

▶When you are crossing a sidewalk to enter a driveway, you must give right-of-way to pedestrians on the sidewalk.

▶You may legally pass on the right if you can pass without driving off the pavement.

▶When you sell or transfer your vehicle to another person, you must report it to DMV within 5 days.

► A solid white line painted on the outer edge of the road marks the edge of the pavement. You may not drive across the white line to pass another vehicle.

► You may not pass where there is a solid line on your side of the center line (white or yellow).

► You should always stop where the signals are solid red, flashing red, and blacked out.

► When two drivers reach an uncontrolled intersection at the same time the driver on the right goes first.

► A child must NOT be left in a car unless a person at least 12 years of age is in the car with the child.

► When you are crossing a divided highway where there are <u>two</u> stop signs, you must also stop at the <u>second sign</u>.

► A child under 8 years of age or less than 4 feet 9 inches tall must ride in a federally approved safety restraint system. (New law 2012)

► A driver over 18 years of age may send or receive a text message if the vehicle is equipped with hands-free voice-operated equipment.

► Motorcycles must be equipped with federally approved emissions equipment.

► If you see an emergency vehicle stopped on the roadway, you must slow down or move to another lane.

► Minors may not send or receive a text message when driving even if the vehicle is equipped with hands-free voice-controlled equipment.

► If you are involved in an accident in which the damage was $750 or more, you must report it to DMV.

► You may drive across a sidewalk to enter or exit a driveway or an alley.

► A yellow arrow (not flashing) means the light is about to change. Be prepared to stop.

► You may not pass another vehicle when there is a solid line on your side of the center line.

► You should always stop where the signal lights are solid red, flashing red, and blacked out.

► When you are crossing a sidewalk to enter a driveway, you must yield (give) right-of-way to pedestrians on the sidewalk.

► When you are crossing a divided highway where there are two stop signs, you must always also stop at the second stop sign.

► If red lights are flashing at an intersection, you must STOP and then proceed with caution.

► You should allow extra space in front of your car when you are following a large bus or any other large vehicle.

►It is your responsibility to know how your medications affect your driving, not your pharmacist's responsibility.

►It is illegal for anyone to smoke in a car where a minor is in the car.

►Children under 8 years of age and less than 4 feet 9 inches tall must ride in a federally approved child-passenger safety restraint system.

► It is illegal to leave a child under 6 years old in a car unless a person at least 12 years old is in the car.

ANSWERS TO PRACTICE TEST No. 1

1. When there is a **minor** in the car
2. May **not** talk on a cell phone while driving
3. They are operated with natural gas or electric powertrains
4. The vehicle has hands-free and voice-operated equipment
5. The vehicle is equipped with a hands-free device
6. Be equipped with federally-required emissions equipment
7. Ride in a federally approved safety restraint system
8. Are in a collision in which there was an injury or a death
9. Except to contact law enforcement in an emergency
10. $750
11. You may be fined up to $1000
12. Call 911 or CHP (California Highway Patrol)
13. Within 5 days
14. DMV may suspend your license
15. Are driving illegally
16. 20/200 or worse
17. More than one vehicle
18. Is attended by a person 12 years of age or older
19. Proof of insurance, vehicle registration, and address
20. Your driving privilege will be revoked for 2 years
21. One year in county jail
22. It may be impounded (taken away) for 30 days
23. Stop again at the second stop sign
24. Solid red lights. Flashing red lights. Blacked out traffic signals.
25. You **cannot** turn against a red arrow, even if you stop first
26. Do as if the intersection were controlled by stop signs
27. Proceed (go ahead) when it is **safe** to do so
28. You may not make a Right Turn
29. Pedestrian Crossing ahead
30. Give right of way to other drivers
31. Near a school
32. You may stop in the area for a while
33. Slow down. Look for trains. Be prepared to stop
34. **Stop**, check traffic in all directions and then go ahead
35. You may not make a U-TURN
36. Be secured in a federally-approved safety restraint system

CALIFORNIA SPEED LIMITS

You must know California's maximum and special speed limits, even if no speed limit signs are posted.

 At a safety zone or an intersection where a trolley or bus is stopped , *and* traffic is controlled by an officer or a traffic signal, the safe passing speed is no more than 10 miles an hour.

 "Blind intersections," where you cannot see 100 feet in either direction before crossing. At a railroad crossing, where you cannot see the track for 400 feet in each direction. In an alley

 School zones. But speeds as low as **15 mph may be posted.**

 On two-lane road-ways
On other roads where that speed is posted

 On most California highways, except for two-lane undivided highways

 On freeways, but only where that speed is posted.

PRACTICE TEST No. 2

RIGHT-OF-WAY LAWS

1. You should give up legal right-of-way:
□ When it would help prevent an accident
□ To all cross traffic
□ To all buses and trucks

Answer: _____

2. If you always insist on letting other drivers go ahead of you at intersections, you are:
□ Most likely causing traffic delays
□ Using defensive driving techniques
□ Improving traffic flow

Answer: _____

PEDESTRIAN SIGNALS

3. Where an intersection or crosswalk has signals to direct pedestrians while crossing the street, the picture of a "RAISED HAND" means:

□ It is safe to cross the street
□ You may not cross the street
□ All vehicles must stop

Answer: _____

Pedestrians <u>do not</u> always have the right of way. Crossing the street against an "Up-Raised Hand" is illegal. You may be given a ticket for it.

4. A light flashing at a crosswalk means:

☐ You may not have time to make it across
☐ You must wait for all traffic to stop
☐ An emergency vehicle is approaching

Answer: _____

5. When a pedestrian signal shows a picture of a "WALKING PERSON":

☐ It is legal to start crossing the street
☐ You may not cross the street
☐ Pedestrians must yield to motor vehicles

Answer: _____

"Pedestrians have responsibilities also. You get hit you say, *"But I had the right-of-way!"* Right-of-way is no good to you when you're trussed up in a hospital bed with a broken head, or worse.

6. Where there are traffic signals but <u>no</u> pedestrian signals, what should pedestrians do?

☐ Go ahead and cross. Pedestrians always have the right-of-way
☐ Obey the red, yellow or green signal lights
☐ Cross on the flashing yellow light

Answer: _____

7.You must give right-of-way to persons using a white cane or a guide dog:

☐ At all times
☐ Only when they are crossing on a red light
☐ Only when they are in a crosswalk

Answer: _____

Do not talk to or pet a guide dog. Do not give a blind pedestrian verbal directions.

8. Pedestrians using white canes or guide dogs use the sound of your engine as a guide. You should stop no more than:

☐ 5 feet from the crosswalk
☐ 3 feet from the crosswalk
☐ 10 feet from the crosswalk

Answer: _____

9. When you are approaching (coming near) a crosswalk where a pedestrian is waiting to cross, you must stop:
☐ The pedestrian is not ready to cross the street
☐ And tell the pedestrian when it is safe to cross the street
☐ And wait until the pedestrian has crossed the street

Answer: _____

INTERSECTIONS and SIGNS

10. This sign is a:

☐ Pedestrian crossing sign
☐ Yield right-of-way sign
☐ School crossing sign

Answer: _____

11. This sign tells you:

☐ There is a traffic light ahead
☐ You are approaching a railroad crossing
☐ There is a school crossing ahead

Answer:_____

12. At an intersection with <u>no</u> STOP or YIELD signs, you must:
□ Obey the STOP sign
□ Yield to the car on your left
□ Slow down, check traffic carefully and then proceed through the intersection

Answer: _____

13. Vehicles turning left on a two-way street must:
□ Yield to oncoming vehicles
□ Yield to vehicles behind them
□ Yield to pedestrians waiting for the WALK signal

Answer: _____

14. When a driver stops ahead of you at a crosswalk, you must:
□ Speed up and pass the driver
□ Change lanes and pass the driver
□ Stop, until all pedestrians have crossed the street

Answer: _____

When a vehicle ahead of you has stopped at a crosswalk, do not attempt to pass the vehicle. A pedestrian is probably in the crosswalk.

15. At intersections, crosswalks and railroad crossings you must always:
□ Come to a complete stop
□ Look to the sides of your vehicle
□ Look straight ahead

Answer: _____

16. Unless another speed is posted, the speed limit on the freeway is:

☐ 70 miles an hour

☐ 65 miles an hour

☐ 55 miles an hour

Answer: _____

17. When may you drive faster than 15 mph in an alley?

☐ NEVER

☐ When another car is chasing you

☐ When you are road-testing your car

Answer: _____

18. California's "basic speed law" means you may:

☐ Not drive faster than is safe for existing conditions

☐ Always drive the posted speed limit

☐ Drive at least 5 miles over the posted speed limit

Answer: _____

19. Broken white lines separate two or more lanes:

☐ In the same direction

☐ In opposite directions

☐ Used for left turns

Answer: _____

20. This sign means you may not:

NO TURN ON RED	☐ Make a right turn on the red light
	☐ Make a U-Turn here
	☐ Park in this space

Answer: _____

21. When approaching a railroad crossing where you cannot see clearly for 400 feet in each direction:
- □ The speed limit is 15 miles per hour (15 mph)
- □ The speed limit is 20 mph
- □ You may drive at least 30 mph

Answer: _____

22. In bad driving conditions the posted speeds:
- □ Must be obeyed
- □ May **not** always be safe
- □ Are always safe

Answer: _____

23. You may not pass a stopped trolley, streetcar or bus in a Safety Zone:
- □ At a speed greater than 15 mph
- □ At a speed greater than 10 mph
- □ Any faster than 15 mph

Answer: _____

24. When a driver behind you wishes to drive faster than you, you should:
- □ Move to the right
- □ Maintain your speed, make him slow down
- □ Drive even slower

Answer: _____

If you cannot move to the right, continue driving the posted speed limit but keep an eye on the driver behind you for any unsafe actions. if he is too close to your bumper tap your brake lights.

25. At a "blind intersection" where you cannot see traffic 100 feet in each direction, the speed limit is:

□ 10 mph
□ 15 mph
□ 20 mph

"BLIND INTERSECTION"

100 feet   100 feet

100 feet

Your vision is blocked by a tree on the left and a building on the right.

Answer: _____

26. You may drive 70mph on the freeway:

□ Only where that speed is posted
□ Anytime
□ Between 10 p.m. and 5 a.m

Answer: _____

27. Unless another speed is posted in a school zone:

□ You may drive no faster than 25 mph
□ You may drive 35 mph
□ You must slow your vehicle to 10 mph

Answer: _____

💡 "Blind intersection" --15mph

28. On a two-lane undivided highway, unless a higher speed is posted, the maximum speed limit is:
□ 55 mph
□ 65 mph
□ 70 mph
Answer: _____

ROAD MARKINGS

29. When there is a solid line on your side of the center line you:
□ May **not** cross over the line to pass another car
□ May cross over it to pass a large, slow truck
□ Must drive much slower

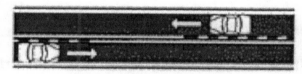

Solid and broken lines

Answer: _____

30. You may cross <u>two</u> solid lines dividing opposite lanes of traffic to:
□ Enter a driveway or turn left at an intersection
□ Pass a driver that is holding up traffic
□ Pass a slow moving farm vehicle

Answer: _____

You may pass on a broken line when it is safe to do so. You may NEVER pass on a solid line unless directed to do so by an officer or a traffic control person.

 Two-lane undivided highway-- 55mph

31. When may you pass on a broken line?
□ Always
□ When it is safe to do so
□ When an oncoming car is 100 feet away

Answer: _____

32. A center left turn lane is to be used to:
□ Pass other vehicles
□ Begin and end left turns, and start a permitted U-turn
□ Make a right turn

Answer: _____

33. When may you pass a car in a left turn center lane?
□ NEVER
□ When a car is barely creeping along
□ When the car is near the right edge of the lane

Answer: _____

Left turn center lanes are for making left turns and for permitted U-Turns.

Before making a U-Turn from a left turn center lane you must check for signs prohibiting (forbidding) U-Turns from that lane.

34. When there are <u>two solid yellow lines</u> dividing traffic going in opposite directions, you may not:
☐ Cross over the lines for any reason
☐ Cross over the lines to make a left turn
☐ Cross over the lines to pass another vehicle

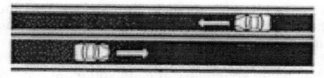

Two solid lines

Answer: _____

35. You may not cross a solid yellow line to:
☐ Pass another car
☐ Make a left turn
☐ Enter or leave a driveway

Answer: _____

36. Unless otherwise posted the speed limit in a school zone is:
☐ 20 mph
☐ 15mph
☐ 25 mph

Answer: _____

If a two-lane undivided highway is posted with a speed limit higher or lower than 55 mph, you may drive at the posted speed <u>when it is safe to do so.</u>

💡 **School zone-- 25mph**

TRUE STATEMENTS

▶ When a blind person takes a step back and pulls in his cane, he is not ready to cross the street. You may proceed (go ahead), but with caution.

▶ When a blind person is in a crosswalk, you should stop within 5 feet of the crosswalk. He or she is guided by the sound of the car's engine.

▶The "basic speed law" means you must not drive faster than is safe for existing conditions.

▶ A left turn center lane is for beginning and ending left turns.

▶ You may <u>not</u> pass a car in a left-turn center lane.

▶ You must stop before making a right turn on a red light. However, if a yield sign is in place, and you will not be taking any other vehicle's legal right-of-way, you may make the turn without stopping.

▶ You may not cross over a solid yellow line to pass another vehicle.

▶ If the line on your side of the center line is broken, you may pass another vehicle when it is safe to do so.

▶ Two solid yellow lines mean "no passing from either direction."

▶The speed limit on a two-lane undivided highway is 55 miles per hour, unless another speed is posted.

▶The speed limit on the freeway is 65 miles per hour unless another speed limit is posted.

ANSWERS TO PRACTICE TEST No. 2

1. When it would help prevent an accident
2. Most likely causing traffic delays
3. You may not cross the street
4. You may not have time to make it across
5. It is legal to start crossing the street
6. Obey the red, yellow or green signals
7. At all times
8. 5 feet from the crosswalk
9. And wait until the pedestrian has crossed the street
10. School crossing sign
11. There is a traffic light ahead
12. Slow down check traffic carefully and then proceed through the intersection
13. Yield to oncoming vehicles
14. Stop, until all pedestrians have crossed the street
15. Look to the sides of your vehicle
16. 65 Miles an hour
17. NEVER
18. **Not** drive faster than is safe for existing conditions
19. In the same direction
20. Make a right turn on the red light
21. 15 miles per hour (15 mph)
22. May **not** always be safe
23. At a speed greater than 10 mph
24. Move to the right
25. 15 mph
26. Only where that speed is posted
27. You may drive no faster than 25 mph
28. 55 mph
29. May **not** cross over it to pass another car
30. Enter a driveway or turn left at an intersection
31. When it is safe to do so
32. Begin and end left turns, and start a permitted U-Turn
33. NEVER
34. Cross over the lines to pass another vehicle
35. Pass another car
36. 25 mph

PRACTICE TEST No. 3

1. You may drive in a CARPOOL lane:
□ When there are two adults and a child in your vehicle
□ When there are two adults and an animal in the vehicle
□ When you are late for work

Answer: _____

RIGHT AND LEFT TURNS

2. You may make a right turn on a red light if there is no sign prohibiting the turn:
□ After making a complete stop
□ Without stopping
□ Only at a very low speed

Answer:_____

3. When making a right turn at a corner, you should start your turn in the right lane and end it in:
□ The far left lane
□ Any lane open to you
□ The lane closest to the curb (the right lane)

Answer: _____

4. This driver is signaling for:

□ A right turn
□ A left turn
□ The driver behind him to slow pass

Answer:_____

U-TURNS

5. U-turns must be made at intersections, or:
☐ From side streets
☐ Where an opening is provided for the turn
☐ In business districts only

Answer: _____

6. You are on a street with <u>two</u> lanes in each direction. To make a U-TURN you should start your turn in
☐ The center left turn lane
☐ Either lane
☐ The left lane

Answer: _____

7. You may not make a U-TURN
☐ In front of a fire station
☐ On a one-way street
☐ Both of the above

Answer: _____

Before making a U-Turn you must be able to see vehicles approaching from either direction from at least 200 feet away.

PARKING ON A HILL

The <u>front wheels</u> of the car determine which way the car will roll. If the front wheels are turned to the left, the rear end of the car will move to the left. If they are turned to the right, the rear end of the car will move to the right.

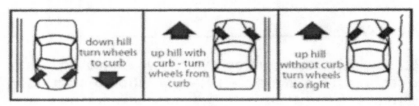

8. You are parking uphill. <u>There is a curb</u>. Turn your wheels:
□ To the Right—toward the side of the road
□ To the Left—toward the center of the road
□ Away from the curb

Answer: _____

9. When you park uphill or downhill with <u>no</u> curb, you should:
□ Turn your wheels toward the side of the road
□ Turn your wheels toward the center of the street
□ Leave your wheels parallel with the curb

Answer: _____

Leave your vehicle in gear or "park" position

10. You have parked on a <u>level</u> street. You should:
□ Turn your wheels to the left
□ Turn your wheels to the right if there is no curb
□ Leave the wheels straight

Answer: _____

PARKING AT COLORED CURBS

11. A curb painted green curb means:
□ Disabled persons may park there
□ No stopping, standing or parking
□ Parking for a limited time (the time posted)

Answer: _____

12. Which vehicle may park at a red curb?
□ A delivery truck
□ A motorcycle
□ A bus (if it is marked for a bus)

Answer: _____

13. A curb painted white means you may stop to:
□ Pick up or drop off passengers or mail
□ Pick up or unload freight
□ Run into the airport and pick up your luggage

Answer: _____

14. You may park at a yellow painted curb but no longer than:
□ The time posted
□ One hour
□ 30 minutes

Answer: _____

15. A curb painted blue means parking for:
□ Disabled persons with special plates or placards
□ Bicycles
□ Motorcycles only

Answer: _____

16. Buses <u>only</u> are permitted to park at:
□ A red zone (for the time posted)
□ White curbs
□ Blue curbs

Answer:_____

17. This sign is posted at a parking space for:

□ Disabled persons with special placards or signs
□ Motorcycles
□ Golf carts

Answer: _____

18. The hand and arm signal for a left turn is:
□ Hand and arm held upward
□ Hand and arm held out, pointing left
□ Hand and arm held downward

Answer: _____

19. It is illegal (against the law) to park:
□ Within 15 feet of a fire hydrant
□ In front of a driveway
□ Both of the above

Answer: _____

20. Double parking is:
□ <u>Illegal</u> at all times
□ Permitted when making deliveries
□ Permitted in school zones

Answer:_____

21. You may <u>not</u> park within_____feet of a sidewalk ramp for disabled persons.
☐ 3
☐ 7 1/2
☐ 15

Answer: _____

22. When you park parallel to a curb (alongside, straight with) your wheels must be no farther from the curb than:
☐ 6 inches
☐ 12 inches
☐ 18 inches

Answer: _____

23. A child less than 4 feet 9 inches must:
☐ Ride in the front seat
☐ Wear a lap and shoulder belt
☐ Ride in a federally approved safety restraint system

Answer: _____

24. Animals may be transported in the back of a truck:
☐ Only when a person is with them
☐ Only when they are properly secured
☐ If you are sure they won't jump out of the truck

Answer: _____

💡 **You must park within <u>18</u> inches of the curb.**

25. Persons riding in the back of a truck must:

□ Ride in a seat and use seat belts
□ Sit on the floor of the truck
□ Stand up and hold on to the sides of the truck bed

Answer: _____

26. When both right and left signals are flashing on the vehicle ahead?

□ You should slow down. There may be a hazard ahead.
□ Speed up and pass it quickly
□ The driver forgot to turn off the signals

Answer: _____

27. A conviction for littering:

□ Will appear on your driving record
□ May cause you to be fined $1000
□ Both of the above

Answer: _____

SIGNALS FOR DRIVERS AND BICYCLISTS

28. Drivers and bicyclists must signal:

□ At least 100 feet before the turn
□ 200 feet before the turn
□ At least 50 feet before the turn

Answer: _____

 Signal <u>100</u> feet before making a turn

29. This is the correct hand and arm signal for:

☐ A right turn
☐ A left turn
☐ Slow or STOP

Answer:_____

30. What kind of hand and arm signal is this?

☐ Slowing or stopping
☐ A left turn
☐ The driver wants to merge with traffic

Answer:_____

31. On sunny days, in addition to your signal lights, you may need to:

☐ Use hand and arm signals
☐ Use your parking lights
☐ Use your headlights

Answer: _____

VISUAL SEARCH/LOOKING AHEAD

At highway speeds, <u>10 to 15 seconds</u> ahead of your vehicle would be about <u>a quarter of a mile</u>. You need to look that far ahead so you can recognize potential dangers and have time to take evasive action. At <u>lower</u> speeds as in city traffic, <u>10 to 15 seconds</u> would be about one block.

●Slow or stop, hand and arm down
● Left turn, hand and arm pointing left
● Right turn, hand and arm pointing straight up

32. To avoid last minute moves, look down the road to where your vehicle will be in about:
□ 10 to 15 seconds
□ 5 to 10 seconds
□ One block

Answer: _____

33. On the <u>highway</u> look ahead of your vehicle:
□ About a quarter of a mile
□ A full block away
□ One-half block

Answer:_____

34. In a <u>city</u> you should <u>not</u> start across an intersection with no traffic controls unless approaching traffic is at least:
□ A half-mile away
□ Half a block away
□ A full block away

Answer: _____

35. It is illegal to enter an intersection when:
□ The light is yellow
□ The light is green
□ You can't get all the way across before the light turns red

Answer: _____

36. "Scanning" means looking <u>ahead</u> of your car:
□ Behind your car and to the sides
□ One full mile
□ One half block

Answer: _____

TRUE STATEMENTS

▶ It is illegal to start across an intersection when you cannot get all the way across before the light changes to red.

▶ At an intersection where no signal lights are working you should proceed as if it were a four-way stop (Stop, check traffic, then go ahead).

▶ A minor can use a cell phone while driving to contact law enforcement, the fire department, or another emergency agency.

▶ U-Turns should be started from the left lane.

▶ Only disabled persons may park at blue curbs.

▶ Anyone riding in the back of a truck must use a seat and seatbelts.

▶ "Scanning" means looking ahead, behind and to the sides of your vehicle.

▶ On the highway look ahead of your vehicle about a quarter of a mile.

▶ In city traffic look ahead of your vehicle one full block.

▶ Right turns should be started in the right lane and ended in the right lane.

▶ Don't start across an intersection unless other traffic is half a block away.

▶ You must not open your door on the traffic side when it would interfere with traffic.

CALIFORNIA'S FINANCIAL RESPONSIBILITY LAW

California drivers must carry the statutory <u>minimum limits</u> of liability insurance as follows

> **$15,000 for a single death or injury in any one accident**

> **$30,000 for death or injury to more than one person in any one accident.**

> **$5,000 for property damage in any one accident.**

California Department of Motor Vehicles will not register a vehicle or issue a license plate without proof of financial responsibility. There is a heavy fine for operating a motor vehicle when you are not covered by liability insurance. You must carry written, or other evidence of financial responsibility whenever you drive. You must show it to a police officer when asked.

Types of Financial Responsibility

- **Motor vehicle liability insurance policy**
- **Cash deposit of $35,000 with DMV**
- **DMV-issued self- insurance policies**
- **Surety bond for $35,000 from a company licensed to do business in California**

ANSWERS TO PRACTICE TEST No. 3

1. When there are two adults and a child in the car
2. After making a complete stop
3. The lane closest to the curb (the right lane)
4. A left turn
5. Where an opening is provided for the turn
6. The left lane
7. Both of the above
8. Away from the curb
9. Turn your wheels toward the side of the road
10. Leave the wheels straight
11. Parking for a limited time (the time posted)
12. A bus (if it is marked for a bus)
13. Pick up or drop off passengers or mail
14. The time posted
15. Disabled persons with special plates or placards
16. A red zone (for the time posted)
17. Disabled persons with special placards or signs
18. Hand and arm held out, pointing left
19. Both of the above
20. Illegal at all times
21. 3 feet
22. 18 inches
23. Ride in a federally approved safety restraint system
24. Only when they are properly secured
25. Ride in a seat and use seat belts
26. You should slow down. There may be a hazard ahead
27. Both of the above
28. 100 feet before the turn
29. A right turn
30. Slow or stopping
31. Use hand and arm signals
32. 10 to 15 seconds
33. About a quarter of a mile
34. Half a block away
35. You can't get all the way across before the light turns red
36. Behind your car and to the sides

PRACTICE TEST No. 4

1. Before entering an intersection, you should look:
□ Right, left, and right again
□ Left, right, and left again
□ Only to the left

Answer:_____

2. When your view at an intersection is blocked:
□ Pull into the intersection slowly
□ Edge forward slowly until you can see cross traffic
□ Blow your horn and go ahead

Answer: _____

3. This sign means you are approaching:

□ A school crossing
□ A pedestrian crossing
□ A visually impaired person in a crosswalk

Answer: _____

4. Pedestrian crosswalks are often marked with:
.□ Red lines
□ White lines
□ Green lines

Answer: _____

SHARROW

This is a SHARROW. It designates lanes that   may   be   shared   by bicyclists and motor vehicles.

5. When making a right turn at a green light, you must watch for persons about to cross the street. They also have:
☐ A green light
☐ A yellow light
☐ A red light

Answer: _____

6. Pedestrians have right-of-way in a crosswalk:
☐ Whether or not the crosswalk is marked
☐ Only if it is painted with white lines
☐ Only if they allow motor vehicles to go first

Answer: _____

When crossing the street, and in parking lots, pedestrians should look around for hybrid and electric vehicles. They are almost silent when operating.

7. By checking behind your vehicle often, you will know:
☐ If you are being crowded by a tailgater
☐ If your vehicle is in the proper lane
☐ If your brake lights are working

Answer: _____

8. You may you not drive using only your parking lights:
☐ Except in the daytime
☐ Except when you are following another vehicle
☐ Under any circumstances

Answer: _____

9. Before changing lanes, you should always:
□ Check traffic beside and behind you
□ Check traffic beside you
□ Check traffic behind you

Answer: _____

10. Glance over your shoulders before changing lanes:
□ So you can see vehicles in your "blind" spots
□ So you can see vehicles that are following too closely
□ So you can see vehicles entering your road

Answer: _____

11. Before backing up, you should:
□ Check behind your vehicle for children and pets
□ Open your window and look down at the pavement
□ Give a left signal

Answer: _____

12. Clear ice, frost or dew from your windows:
□ Before you drive
□ After you get out of your driveway
□ In the daytime only

Answer: _____

13. Adjust the seat, mirrors, and safety belt:
□ Before starting the car
□ After starting the car
□ So you can see the left rear bumper

Answer: _____

14. If your license says you must wear "corrective lenses," and you are caught driving without them:
□ You may be fined
□ Your license may be revoked
□ You will have to take a driving test

Answer: _____

15. You are driving in the rain and fog. Your wipers are working but you still cannot see the road ahead. You should:
□ Slow down and turn on your low beam lights
□ Turn on your headlights
□ Pull off the road until visibility improves

Answer: _____

16. When visibility* is bad due to rain, snow or fog, to make sure other drivers see you:
□ Turn on your parking lights
□ Turn on your high beam headlights
□ Turn on your low-beam lights

Answer: _____

Visibility*: the distance you can see ahead of your vehicle

17. If your vehicle starts to lose traction because of water on the road (hydroplanes), you should:
□ Slow down gradually and **not** apply the brakes
□ Use your high beam headlights
□ Use your parking lights

Answer: _____

18. If the fog is so thick you cannot see:
□ Turn on your high beams so you can see
□ Pull completely off the road and stop
□ Turn on your "parking" lights

Answer: _____

19. Motorcycles are harder to see at night:
□ Because they have only one taillight
□ Because they have only one headlight
□ Because they don't have any brake lights

Answer: _____

20. The law says you must turn on your headlights 30 minutes after sunset and leave them on until:
□ 30 minutes before sunrise
□ 9 a.m.
□ The smog clears

Answer: _____

21. At night you must switch to low beam headlights:
□ Within 500 feet of an oncoming vehicle
□ When you are on a narrow country road
□ When you are within 1,000 feet of an oncoming vehicle

Answer: _____

22. When driving behind another vehicle at night, you should use you low beam headlights:
□ When you are within 300 feet of the vehicle
□ When you are within 500 feet of the vehicle
□ When the vehicle ahead flashes its brake lights

Answer: _____

23. When oncoming headlights bother you:

□ Look at the center line of the street
□ Close your eyes for a few seconds
□ Look at the right edge of the road

Answer: _____

24. A vehicle coming toward you has only one light, you should drive to the right as far as possible:

□ It may be a car with a missing headlight
□ It probably has a bad driver
□ The driver may be drunk

Answer: _____

25. Low beam headlights most often are used for city driving, and driving in the rain, fog or snow. You should also use them when:

□ Driving on narrow country roads in the daytime
□ Driving on very dark highways
□ You can only see 100 feet ahead of your vehicle

Answer: _____

26. This sign is orange-colored. It means slow down:

□ There is a slow moving vehicle ahead
□ There are workmen ahead
□ You must stop

Answer: _____

Look to the right edge of the road when oncoming headlights bother you.

27. You should use your headlights anytime:

☐ You are driving in the city
☐ You have trouble seeing other cars
☐ You want other drivers to move to the right lane

Answer: _____

28. If your car breaks down, pull completely off the road:

☐ And turn on your emergency flashers
☐ And turn on your headlights
☐ And open your car doors

Answer: _____

29. You are on a highway with two traffic lanes in your direction. A vehicle has stopped on the right shoulder of the road ahead with its hazard lights on, you should:

☐ Change lanes to the left and speed up
☐ Let drivers behind you know they should stop
☐ Slow down and pass carefully

Answer: _____

30. Check your turn signal <u>after</u> making a turn:

☐ And turn it off if it didn't go off
☐ And make sure it stays on for at least 100 feet
☐ And slow down

Answer: _____

Always check your turn signal after making a turn.

31. At highway speeds you should signal at least 5 seconds:

□ Before changing lanes
□ Before stopping
□ After you have changed lanes

Answer: _____

32. Before changing lanes you should:

□ Check your mirrors and look over your shoulder
□ Only check your mirrors.
□ Signal at least 50 feet

Answer: _____

THREE-SECOND FOLLOWING RULE

Most rear-end collisions are caused by following too closely. When the car ahead of you passes a definite mark such as a building or a sign, start counting "one thousand and one, one thousand and two, one thousand and three." This takes about 3 seconds. If you reach the sign before you finish counting, you are following too closely.

33. If you rear-ended a car, you were probably:

□ Following too closely
□ Passing in the wrong lane
□ Driving too slowly

Answer: _____

34. You may need more than a "3-second space cushion" when you are:
☐ Being crowded by a tailgater
☐ Traveling slower than the speed limit
☐ Transporting animals in your vehicle

Answer:_____

35. If you drive to the scene of an accident just to take a look:
☐ You may be of some assistance
☐ You must stop at least 10 feet from the scene
☐ You may be arrested

Answer: _____

36. Two of the most common causes of accidents are unsafe speed and:
☐ Always giving up your right-of-way
☐ Increasing your following distance
☐ Driving on the wrong side of the road

Answer: _____

MORE TRUE STATEMENTS

►Orange construction signs mean you must slow down for road workers and slow moving equipment ahead.

►It is illegal to use the unpaved portion of the road to pass a car making a left turn

►When you need to back up, you should check behind your vehicle for children and pets.

►Before changing lanes you should check traffic beside and behind you.

► Using low beam headlights on narrow country roads during the day helps other drivers see you.

►When oncoming headlights bother you, you should look to the right side of the road.

►You must switch to low beam headlights when you are within 500 feet of an oncoming vehicle.

► When following another vehicle, switch to low beams when you are within 300 feet of the vehicle.

► Highways are most slippery immediately after the rain starts.

► If your car loses traction because of water on the road (hydroplanes), you should slow down gradually and not apply the brakes.

► To check your blind spots, look over your right shoulder when changing to a right lane and over your left shoulder when changing to a left lane.

►When yielding to an emergency vehicle, do not stop in an intersection.

►You should turn on your windshield wipers and headlights on rainy, snowy or foggy days so other drivers can see you.

► You may not stop a passenger vehicle next to a red-painted curb (at any time).

ANSWERS TO PRACTICE TEST No. 4

1. Left, right and left again
2. Edge forward slowly until you can see cross traffic
3. A pedestrian crossing
4. White lines
5. A green light
6. Whether or not the crosswalk is marked
7. If you are being crowded by a tailgater
8. Under any circumstances
9. Check traffic beside and behind you
10. So you can see vehicles in your "blind" spots
11. Check behind your vehicle for children and pets
12. Before you drive
13. Before starting the car
14. Your license may be revoked
15. Pull off the road until visibility improves
16. Turn on your low beam headlights
17. Slow down gradually and **not** apply the brakes
18. Pull completely off the road and stop
19. Because they have only one taillight
20. 30 minutes before sunrise
21. Within 500 feet of an <u>oncoming</u> vehicle
22. When you are within 300 feet of the vehicle
23. Look at the right edge of the road
24. It may be a car with a missing headlight
25. Driving on narrow country roads in the daytime
26. There is a slow moving vehicle ahead
27. You have trouble seeing other cars
28. And turn on your emergency flashers
29. Slow down and pass carefully
30. And turn it off if it didn't go off
31. Before changing lanes
32. Check your mirrors and look over your shoulder
33. Following too closely
34. Being crowded by a tailgater
35. You may be arrested
36. Driving on the wrong side of the road

PRACTICE TEST No. 5

1. When following a large vehicle that blocks your view, you need extra room to:
□ Keep out of the vehicle's way
□ See around the vehicle
□ See its brake lights

Answer: _____

2. If another driver cuts in front of you:
□ Blow your horn to let the driver know you are angry
□ Take your foot off the gas, make a larger "space cushion" (in front of you)
□ Speed up so the driver can't return to your lane

Answer: _____

3. If you drive in another driver's blind spot:
□ The driver may change lanes and hit you
□ You may be arrested for following too closely
□ You may be rear-ended by another vehicle

Answer: _____

4. Don't drive too close to parked cars:
□ A car door may suddenly open
□ A car may suddenly pull out in front of you
□ Both of the above

Answer: _____

5. You should slow down for drivers who:
□ Pass you as you approach a curve or oncoming cars
□ Are rude to you
□ Are coming toward you in the opposite lane

Answer: _____

6. If you are being followed by a tailgater, you should tap your brake lights:
□ To show the driver that you don't like it
□ As a warning before you slow down
□ To increase your following distance

Answer: _____

7. A car is coming toward you on the left and a child on a bike is on your right. You should:
□ Let the car pass, move to the left and pass the child on the bike
□ Honk your horn and pass the child
□ Honk your horn and quickly pass the car

Answer: _____

8. Watch for drivers who may be confused. If you see a driver in trouble:
□ Do what you can to help him or her out
□ Maintain your speed so they will get off the road
□ Get "even" with the driver by not slowing down at all

Answer: _____

 Tap your brake lights to warn a tailgater when you when you are about to slow down

SEAT BELTS/SAFETY BELTS

9. You must wear your seat belt:
☐ Unless the vehicle is equipped with airbags
☐ Unless you are riding in a large truck
☐ If the vehicle is equipped with seat belts.

Answer: _____

Ladies, slip the passenger-side seat belt through the handle of your purse. If you should have an accident your purse will stay with the car.

10. Can you be given a traffic ticket if a passenger 15 years or younger is not wearing a seat belt?
☐ Yes
☐ No
☐ Only if he or she is sitting in the back seat

Answer: _____

11. Seat belts:
☐ Save lives
☐ Usually hold you in the car when there is a collision
☐ Both of the above

Answer:_____

12. Any child <u>over</u> 4 feet 9 inches tall:
☐ May wear an appropriate safety belt
☐ May not ride in the rear seat
☐ Must ride in a federally approved child-passenger safety restraint system

Answer: _____

13. Who must ride in the rear seat in a rear-facing safety restraint system?
□ Babies weighing less than 20 pounds
□ Children over 40 pounds
□ Children over six years of age

Answer: _____

MERGING/CROSSING/EXITING/PASSING

14. When entering the freeway your speed should be:
□ About 35 miles per hour
□ At or near the same speed as freeway traffic
□ 55 miles per hour

Answer: _____

15. If you have to cross several lanes on the freeway:
□ Take them one at a time
□ Use your signal for each lane change
□ Both of the above

Answer: _____

Turn on your signal, enter a lane, turn off your signal. Drive about 100 feet. Turn on your signal, enter the next lane, turn off your signal. Do this until you are in the lane you want.

16. Do not stop before merging with freeway traffic:
□ Unless you are driving a large truck
□ Unless it is absolutely necessary
□ Unless there is no traffic close behind you

Answer: _____

17. When approaching a hill or a curve, and you do not have a clear view of the road ahead, you should:
□ Slow down so you can stop if necessary
□ Use you high beams lights to be more visible
□ Stay near the center of the road so you can see oncoming traffic

Answer: _____

18. You must not drive off the paved portion of the road:
□ Unless an officer directs you to
□ Unless you need to pass a slow-moving vehicle
□ Except to pass a bicyclist

Answer: _____

19. This sign means:

PASS
WITH
CARE

□ Do not pass at any time
□ You must make sure it is safe to pass
□ You are approaching a "turnout" lane

Answer: _____

20. You may pass on the right if:
□ There are two or more left turn lanes
□ There are two or more lanes going in your direction
□ There are cars in the left lane

Answer: _____

21. When passing another vehicle, it is safe to return to your lane when you:

□ Can see the vehicle's left rear door
□ See the vehicle's headlights in your rearview mirror
□ You have passed the vehicle's left fender

Answer: _____

22. You are driving on a two-lane road (one lane in each direction) and want to pass another vehicle. You must:

□ Not Pass
□ Not pass until it is safe to do so
□ Not pass until the driver in front of you signals it is safe to pass

Answer: _____

DON'T ALWAYS TRUST OTHER DRIVER'S SIGNALS

Don't always trust another driver's signal that it is OK for you to do something. A driver in front of you may have seen you trying to pass, feel there is enough clear space ahead for you to pass safely and signal for you to go ahead and pass him. The driver doesn't know your capabilities, how fast you drive, if you can make it safely. Wait until you are sure you can pass safely. If the vehicle coming toward you is close enough for you to tell that it is moving closer to you, it is probably too close for you to start to pass.

You want to make a right turn. A car on your left is blocking your vision. The driver of the car on your left can see what's coming and may signal that it is OK for you to go ahead and make a right turn. See for yourself if it is safe. Keep edging toward the street until you can see around the car on your left.

23. It is especially dangerous to pass another vehicle:
□ At intersections
□ Railroad crossings and shopping center entrances
□ Both of the above

Answer: _____

24. You may not pass another vehicle when:
□ The yellow line on your side of the center line is broken
□ There is a solid line on your side of the center line
□ Oncoming traffic is more than one-third of a mile away

Answer: _____

25. You may pass another vehicle if:
□ The yellow line on your side of the center line is broken
□ The driver ahead of you signals it is OK to pass
□ There is a solid line on your side of the center line

Answer: _____

26. On a one-lane mountain road:
□ The car going downhill has right of way
□ The car going uphill has right of way
□ The car with its lights on has right of way

Answer: _____

27. When approaching a sharp curve in the road:
□ Brake before you enter the curve
□ Brake to slow down after you enter the curve
□ Accelerate (speed up) before you enter the curve

Answer: _____

28. To exit (leave) the freeway safely, you should:
□ Signal approximately 5 seconds before the exit
□ Slow down as soon as you get in the exit lane
□ Stay in the #2 lane until you are almost ready to exit

Answer: _____

29. This sign means:

□ Yield (give) right-of-way to other drivers
□ Give right-of-way to drivers behind you
□ Make a complete stop then go ahead

Answer:_____

30. The "implied consent" law means you have agreed to take a test for alcohol or drugs in your body:
□ Any time you drive in California
□ Only upon the advice of your attorney
□ When your doctor tells you to

Answer: _____

31. If you become sleepy while driving you should:
□ Drive slower
□ Drive to a safe place and rest
□ Move into the right lane

Answer: _____

32. If you rear-ended a car, you were probably:
□ Following too closely
□ Passing in the wrong lane
□ Driving too slowly

Answer: _____

33. A drivers going downhill must <u>yield</u> to a driver going uphill
☐ Because a driver has better control of a vehicle when backing uphill
☐ Because the driver going uphill may not see you
☐ Because the driver going downhill is a better driver

Answer: _____

Identify the signs below:

34._____

35._____

36._____

 Signal 5 seconds before exiting the freeway

TRUE STATEMENTS

▶ If you drive too close to parked cars, a car may suddenly pull out in front of you.

▶ If you are being followed by a tailgater, tap your brake lights before you slow down.

▶ If a passenger in your car is 15 years or younger and not wearing a seat belt, you may be given a ticket.

▶Vehicles towing another vehicle on the freeway must travel in either of the two right lanes.

▶ You must not drive off the paved portion of the road unless a road worker or an officer directs you to.

▶ Passing on a solid yellow line is illegal and unsafe.

▶ You may pass on a yellow broken line when it is safe to do so.

▶Signal at least 5 seconds before exiting the freeway.

▶ Signal at least 5 seconds before changing lanes on the freeway.

▶ If another driver cuts in front of you, take your foot off the gas to make a larger "space cushion."

▶When following a large vehicle, you need extra room to see around it.

►Babies should not ride in the front seat in vehicles equipped with passenger-side air bags.

►You must <u>not</u> stop before merging with freeway traffic unless it is absolutely necessary.

►If you become sleepy while driving, you should drive to a safe place and rest.

►The law requires that you <u>not</u> leave your vehicle until you have turned off the engine and set the parking brake.

► A person under 21 years of age who drives with a blood alcohol content (BAC) of 0.01% is driving illegally.

► A drug that makes you drive unsafely is illegal, even a prescription drug.

► Driving with your headlights on will help others to see you on narrow country roads.

► A vehicle going downhill must yield to a vehicle going uphill.

► It is illegal to take any drug before driving that makes you sleepy.

► You must use your seat belt if the vehicle is equipped with seat belts.

► Tank trucks marked with hazardous materials placards must stop at railroad crossings.

ANSWERS TO PRACTICE TEST No. 5

1. See around the vehicle
2. Take your foot off the gas and make a larger "space cushion" (in front of you)
3. The driver may change lanes and hit you
4. Both of the above
5. Pass you as you approach a curve or oncoming car
6. As a warning before you slow down
7. Let the car pass, move to the left and pass the child on the bike
8. Do what you can to help him out
9. If the vehicle is equipped with seat belts
10. Yes
11. Both of the above
12. May wear an appropriate safety belt
13. Babies weighing less than 20 pounds
14. At about the same speed as freeway traffic
15. Both of the above
16. Unless it is absolutely necessary
17. Slow down so you can stop, if necessary
18. Unless an officer directs you to
19. You must make sure it is safe to pass
20. There are two or more lanes going in your direction
21. Can see the vehicle's headlights in your rearview mirror
22. Not pass until it is safe to do so
23. Both of the above
24. When there is a <u>solid</u> line on your side of the center line
25. The yellow line on your side of the center line is broken
26. The car going uphill has right of way
27. Brake before you enter the curve
28. Signal approximately five seconds before the exit
29. Yield (give) right-of-way to other drivers
30. Any time you drive in California
31. Drive to a safe place and rest
32. Following too closely
33. Because a driver has control when backing uphill
34. Keep Right
35. Side Road
36. Left Turns Only

PRACTICE TEST No. 6

LARGE TRUCKS AND BUSES

1. You are following a large truck or bus. You are in the truck's blind spot if:
□ You can't see the truck's side mirrors
□ You can't see the truck's rearview mirror
□ You are passing the truck's left front fender

Answer: _____

2. How should you pass a large truck?
□ Pass quickly in the left lane
□ Pass quickly in the right lane
□ Pass slowly and carefully

Answer: _____

Ninety eight percent of deaths in truck-passenger vehicle accidents are <u>occupants of the smaller passenger vehicles.</u>

Don't attempt to pass a large truck unless you are sure you can pass safely. Once alongside it you may discover that it is traveling much faster than you thought.

<u>Don't linger beside a truck</u>. Either go ahead and pass it or move back in behind it. Some truck drivers drive many hours without sleep and are not always safely alert and may swerve into your lane.

When you meet a large truck, <u>stay closer to the right edge of your lane</u> to prevent a side-swipe. Keep firm control of the steering wheel. Wind turbulence can push your vehicle off the road.

3. A large truck is giving a left signal. Which side should you pass on?

☐ The right side

☐ The left side

☐ You should not pass until you see if the truck is going to turn right or left

Answer: _____

A truck may be giving a left signal because it has to swing over into the left lane to have enough space in which to make a right turn.

(Illustration from Florida Driver's Handbook)

4. Large trucks turning right onto a street with two lanes in each direction:

☐ Must complete their turn in the right lane

☐ Must complete their turn in the left lane

☐ May complete their turn in either the left or right lane

Answer: _____

SCHOOL BUSES

5. Flashing yellow lights on a school bus mean:

☐ The bus is preparing to stop

☐ The bus is about to pass you

☐ It is safe to pass the bus

Answer: _____

6. When a school bus has stopped <u>ahead</u> of you with red lights flashing, you must:
□ Stop as long as the red lights are flashing
□ Stop, then proceed when safe
□ Stop until all children are off the bus

Answer: _____

7. You are traveling on a divided highway <u>behind</u> a school bus with red lights flashing. Must you stop behind it?
□ Yes
□ No
□ Only if there are children on the bus

Answer: _____

8. You are traveling on a divided highway with a paved or grassy median strip. A school bus with red lights flashing is stopped on the <u>opposite</u> side of the highway. Do you have to stop?
□ No
□ Yes, if children are being unloaded from the bus
□ Only if the bus is carrying small children

Answer: _____

9. A school bus has stopped on a road with <u>two-way traffic.</u> Which of the following vehicles must stop?
□ Vehicles behind the bus
□ Vehicles approaching the bus
□ Both of the above

Answer: _____

TROLLEYS/ STREET CARS/ BUSES

10. You may not pass a stopped bus or a streetcar at a speed any faster than:
☐ 5 mph
☐ 10 mph
☐ The bus or streetcar is traveling

Answer: _____

11. You must not turn in front of trolleys unless a signal light indicates you may do so, because:
☐ Trolleys **can** preempt (interrupt) traffic signals
☐ You must always yield to trolleys
☐ Trolleys may not interrupt traffic signals

Answer: _____

12. You must not pass a streetcar or trolley on the left except when:
☐ You are on a one-way street
☐ You are on a multilane highway
☐ The trolley is not moving

Answer: _____

13. When you see or hear an emergency vehicle using a siren and red lights, you must:
☐ Drive to the right edge of the road and stop
☐ Stop wherever you are, even in an intersection
☐ Slow down and let it pass

Answer: _____

Do not stop in an intersection. Keep going until you can pull over and let the emergency vehicle pass.

ORDERS FROM POLICE OFFICERS, FIRE FIGHTERS, ROAD WORKERS

14. Must you obey orders from police officers, fire fighters, and signal persons at construction sites, even if the order conflicts with the law?

□ Yes, always
□ Only when a signal is not working
□ Only if they are holding a stop sign

Answer: _____

15. Must you obey a crossing guard at a school crossing?

□ Yes
□ Yes, but only if she is wearing a uniform
□ No

Answer: _____

16. When you see orange-colored construction signs on a roadway, you must:
□ Change lanes and maintain your speed
□ Exit the roadway as soon as possible
□ Slow down for workers and slow moving equipment

Answer:_____

Fines are doubled for some violations where road workers are present.

17. You should be alert for the triangular orange-colored signs attached to the back of farm tractors and animal drawn vehicles. These vehicles:

- □ Often travel 25 mph or less
- □ Always travel in the left lane
- □ Must pull off the road and let you pass

Answer: _____

MOTORCYCLES AND BICYCLES

18. Which of these vehicles is entitled to share the road with you?

- □ Motorcycles and bicycles
- □ Motorized wheelchairs, golf carts, scooters, and animal-drawn vehicles
- □ All of the above

Answer: _____

19. Motorcycles are entitled to use:

- □ Only one-half of a lane
- □ A full lane
- □ Sirens or whistles

Answer: _____

20. When turning right or left, you must look carefully for motorcycles. One may:

- □ Be in your blind spot
- □ Be following too closely
- □ Not have its headlight on

Answer: _____

21. Allow extra space in front of your vehicle when following:
☐ A motorcycle
☐ Two passenger cars
☐ A pickup truck

Answer: _____

22. Before changing lanes or making a left turn, you must look carefully for motorcycles because:
☐ They are hard to see
☐ They have the right-of-way
☐ Their drivers cannot see you

Answer: _____

23. When passing a bicyclist riding on the right edge of the lane, you should:
☐ Always change lanes
☐ Stay close to the bicyclist
☐ Allow at least 3 feet between you and the bicyclist

Answer: _____

24. Bicyclist must travel:
☐ In the same direction as other traffic
☐ In specially marked bicycle lanes only
☐ On the side of the road, off the pavement

Answer: _____

Bicyclists may ride in the same lane as automobiles , but should ride near the right edge of the roadway. Bicyclists must not ride on the sidewalk. Bicyclists should wear bike helmets with the strap fastened, bright clothing, sneakers, or shoes with heels, and no flip-flops. Helmets and bikes should have reflectors.

TRAIN CROSSINGS

25. You are approaching a railroad crossing. You don't see any flashing lights or hear any bells ringing. You should:

☐ Look both ways and be ready to stop, if necessary
☐ Hurry across the track
☐ Stop

This sign is posted <u>at</u> the railroad tracks

Answer: _____

26. When red lights are flashing at a railroad crossing, how far must you stop from the tracks?
☐ At least 15 feet from the nearest track.
☐ 7 1/2 feet from the nearest track
☐ 50 feet from the nearest track

Answer: _____

27. When is it legal for you to go around a <u>closed</u> railroad gate?
☐ When the train is half a mile away
☐ When you hear a train whistle from a long way off
☐ NEVER

Answer: _____

Never stop on the train tracks expecting you'll be able to get across them before a train comes. Stay where you are until traffic on the other side has moved far enough for you to get completely across the tracks. If your car stops on the tracks, get out of it and run away from the train.

28. You may make a U-Turn in a residential area:

☐ Across two solid double yellow lines
☐ On a one-way street at a green arrow
☐ When there are no vehicles close enough to interfere with your U-TURN

Answer: _____

29. You see a sign that has these words on it, "PASSING LANE AHEAD." What does it mean?

☐ You may use the lane to pass another car
☐ NO PASSING
☐ Only slower cars may use the lane to pass

Answer: _____

30. Roadways that freeze first are:

☐ Tunnels
☐ Bridges
☐ Intersections

Answer: _____

31. What does this sign mean?

Two-way Traffic Ahead

☐ Traffic ahead travels in both directions
☐ One-way Street
☐ No Parking anytime

Answer: _____

32. Solid white lines mark traffic lanes:

☐ Going in the same direction
☐ On one-way streets
☐ Both of the above

Answer: _____

33. At a corner where there is a stop sign, you must first stop:
□ At the crosswalk or a white "limit line"
□ At the corner
□ 10 feet from the corner

Answer: _____

34. Parking is <u>not</u> permitted:
□ In a crosshatched space
□ On a sidewalk
□ Both of the above

Answer: _____

35. To avoid skidding on a slippery road, you should:
□ Follow in the tracks of the vehicle ahead of you
□ Slow down as you approach curves and intersections
□ Drive in the right lane only

Answer: _____

36. A safety zone, a space set aside for pedestrians:
□ Is marked by raised buttons or markers on a roadway
□ Is marked with red flags
□ May be used as a place to park bicycles

Answer: _____

 A safety zone marked by raised buttons is a space set aside for pedestrians.

TRUE STATEMENTS

▶If you are on a road with two-way traffic (an undivided road) and are either approaching a stopped school bus or are behind it, you must STOP.

▶On a divided road, on the same side as a stopped school the bus, you must STOP.

▶You must ALWAYS obey orders from police officers, firefighters and signal persons at construction sites, even if it conflicts with the law.

▶A green painted curb means you may stop there for a limited time.

▶A yellow painted curb is for loading and unloading passengers or freight.

▶Large trucks turning right may complete their turn in either the left or right lane

▶Seat belts, properly worn, are required by law.

▶On a divided road, if you are on the opposite side from the bus, you don't need to stop

▶If there is no signal light, you may not turn in front of an approaching trolley.

▶Trolleys can interrupt (preempt) signals.

▶You may not pass a stopped bus or trolley at a speed any faster than 10 miles an hour.

▶A "Safety Zone" is a space set aside for pedestrians.

ANSWERS TO PRACTICE TEST No. 6

1. Can't see the truck's side mirrors
2. Pass quickly in the left lane
3. You should not pass until you see if the truck is going to turn right or left
4. May complete their turn in either the left or right lane
5. The bus is preparing to stop
6. Stop as long as the red lights are flashing
7. Yes
8. No
9. Both of the above
10. 10 mph
11. Trolleys can preempt (interrupt) traffic signals
12. You are on a one-way street
13. Drive to the right edge of the road and stop
14. Yes, always
15. Yes
16. Slow down for workers and slow moving equipment
17. Often travel 25 mph or less
18. All of the above
19. A full lane
20. Be in your blind spot
21. A motorcycle
22. They are hard to see
23. Allow at least 3 feet between you and the bicyclist
24. In the same direction as other traffic
25. Look both ways and be ready to stop, if necessary.
26. At least 15 feet from the nearest track
27. NEVER
28. When there are no vehicles close enough to interfere with your U-Turn
29. You may use the lane to pass another car
30. Bridges
31. Traffic ahead travels in both directions
32. Both of the above
33. At the crosswalk or a white "limit line"
34. Both of the above
35. Slow down as you approach curves and intersections
36. Is marked by raised buttons or markers on a roadway

REVIEW QUESTIONS

1. Accidents are more likely to happen when one driver is going faster than the other driver:
□True
□ False

Answer: _____

SKIDDING

2. If your car goes into a skid, you should ease off the gas and turn your wheels, gently, in the direction of the skid.
□ True
□ False

Answer: _____

3. This sign tells you the road ahead is slippery when wet.

□ True
□ False

Answer: _____

4. When approaching a curve, you should brake before entering the curve.
□ True
□ False

Answer: _____

5. When driving on snow or ice, before going down a steep hill, you should shift to low gear.
□ True
□ False

Answer: _____

6. If you hit a parked car and cannot find the owner, you should leave a note on it with your name and address and immediately report it to the city police or CHP.
□ True
□ Just leave a note on it with your name and address.

Answer: _____

FINANCIAL RESPONSIBILITY

7. California's COMPULSORY FINANCIAL RESPONSIBILITY LAW requires that drivers and owners of motor vehicles carry liability coverage:
□ At all times.
□ To pay for all their car repairs

Answer: _____

Before you drive in California, you should ask your insurance agent if your liability insurance will cover you there.

8. The minimum amount of liability insurance you must carry is: $15,000, $30,000, $5,000.
□ True
□ False

Answer: _____

DRUGS AND ALCOHOL

9. If you are convicted of driving with alcohol or drugs in your body you may be sentenced to 6 months in jail and you may have to pay fine of up to $1000.
□ True
□ False

Answer: _____

10. Prescription medications are always safe to take, even when you drive.
□ True
□ False

Answer: _____

11. Adults may send or receive a text message while driving if their vehicle is equipped with hands-free, voice controlled equipment.
□ True
□ False

Answer: _____

Adults must also use a hands-free device when talking on a cell phone while driving.

12. Fines are doubled for violations in a construction zone while workers are present.
□ False
□ True

Answer: _____

13. A child under 4 feet 9 inches tall must ride in a:
□ A federally- approved safety restraint system
□ A backward-facing child seat

Answer:_____

14. This crosshatched sign is located beside a parking space for disabled persons.

□ True
□ False

Answer: _____

15. Motorcycles must be equipped with federally-approved:
□ Emissions equipment
□ Horns made especially for motorcycles

Answer: _____

16. To stay alert on long trips:
□ Drink some beer or wine
□ Open a window, sing, or pull off the road and rest awhile

Answer: _____

17. When driving in a roundabout you must not stop or pass other vehicles:
□ False
□ True

Answer: _____

18. Is it legal to wear a headset covering both ears while driving?
□ Yes, if you are listening to CDs
□ NO

Answer: _____

19. This lane in the center of the street can be used to make a left turn.

□ True
□ False

Answer:_____

PEDESTRIANS

20. Is it legal to wear ear plugs in both ears while driving?
□ NO
□ Yes, if you don't hear very well

Answer: _____

You may not wear ear plugs in both ears when driving.

ROUNDABOUTS

21. Vehicles entering a roundabout:
☐ Must yield to vehicles, bicycles, and pedestrians
☐ Always have the right of way

Answer: _____

22. When you change lanes or exit the roundabout you:
☐ Must use your turn signals
☐ Must not use your turn signals

Answer: _____

23. A driver over 18 may send or listen to a text message while driving if their vehicle is equipped with:
☐ Hands-free voice-operated equipment
☐ CB radio

Answer: _____

24. This sign tells you if you are being closely followed by 5 or more cars you must:

SLOWER TRAFFIC USE TURNOUTS	☐ Pull into a designated turnout ☐ Maintain your speed so other drivers will obey the speed limit

Answer: _____

25. Which of these statements about roadwork is true?
☐ Fines are doubled for some violations
☐ Road-working equipment is painted white

Answer: _____

26.This sign means:

☐ You must **not** enter the street from your direction
☐ Enter the intersection carefully

Answer: _____

27.When you see this sign, you must go:

◄ ONE WAY

☐ To the left
☐ Straight ahead

Answer: _____

28. When you keep your eyes moving, looking for possible hazards:
☐ You are driving dangerously
☐ You are "scanning" and driving defensively

Answer: _____

aim high in steering
get the big picture
keep your eyes moving
leave yourself an "out"
make sure others see you

"Scanning" is looking ahead, to the sides, and behind your vehicle.

29. Adult drivers may not talk on a cell phone while driving unless the vehicle is equipped with:
☐ A hands-free device
☐ A steering knob on the steering wheel

Answer:_____

30. Drivers under age 18 may not talk on a cell phone while driving:
□ Unless the vehicle is equipped with a hands-free device
□ Except for emergency purposes

Answer:_____

31. When approaching a roadside emergency along a state highway, drivers must:
□ Move over and slow down
□ Stop, until the emergency vehicle leaves the area

Answer:_____

32. A driver under 18 may not send or listen to a text message while driving:
□ Even if the vehicle is equipped with hands-free, voice-operated equipment
□ Unless a person 25 years old is in the vehicle

Answer:_____

Drivers under age 18:
•No texting
•No cell phone use (except in an emergency situation)

ANSWERS TO REVIEW QUESTIONS

1. True
2. True
3. True
4. True
5. True
6. True
7. At all times
8. True
9. True
10. False
11. True
12. True
13. Federally-approved safety restraint system
14. True
15. Emissions equipment
16. Open a window, sing, or pull off the road and rest
17. True
18. NO
19. True
20. NO
21. Must yield to vehicles, bicycles and pedestrians
22. Must use your turn signals
23. Hands-free, voice-operated equipment
24. Pull into a turnout
25. Fines are doubled for some violations
26. You must not enter the street from your direction
27. To the left
28. You are "scanning" and driving defensively
29. A hands-free device
30. Except for emergency purposes
31. Move over and slow down
32. Even if the vehicle is equipped with hands-free, voice-operated equipment

That's it! No more questions. If you pass the written test, and you don't have to take a behind-the-wheel driving test, you will need to have your vision tested and a picture taken. See "The Photo Shoot" page 93.

If you are taking a behind-the-wheel test, your picture will not be taken until you pass the behind-the-wheel test.

THE VISION TEST

CALIFORNIA VISION EXAM REQUIREMENTS

DMV's vision screening standard is:

- 20/40 with both eyes tested together

- 20/40 in one eye and

- 20/70 at least, in the other eye

If you wear eyeglasses, be sure to bring them to the licensing office. If you are wearing contact lenses, you will not be asked to remove them.

You may be tested by reading letters on a wall chart. If you can't read the wall chart, you will be asked to look into a vision testing machine for specific objects. If you can't pass either vision test, you may be required to take a behind-the-wheel driving test to determine if you can compensate for your vision problems.

If you don't pass either vision exam, you may be referred to a vision specialist who will probably prescribe eye glasses, or a stronger prescription for the eye glasses you are currently wearing.

THE PHOTO SHOOT

Some DMV cameras don't take very good pictures but there are ways to keep your picture from looking like an America's Most Wanted Mug Shot.

Wear some color next to your face. White may make you look washed out. Ladies, arrange your hair and touch up your makeup before you get in line to have that *lovely* picture taken. Don't ask the examiner to wait while you do it there.

Relax. Don't raise your chin and assume a "boot camp" stance. If the camera is lower than your face, it may distort your features. Stand in a relaxed position. Look into the camera lens. Smile if you like, but try not to blink your eyes.

If you have to wear glasses when you drive, you may have to leave them on while your picture is taken. If they are for reading only, you may take them off. If you are wearing contact lenses, tell the camera person.

DRIVERS UNDER 21

Teen drivers: You can probably hold your car in the road at NASCAR speeds. Your reaction time and reflexes are better than that of most older drivers, but you have one big disadvantage—inexperience. Your quick reactions can't totally compensate for your lack of skill and judgment.

It takes years to develop adequate maneuvering skills. And judgment can only come from years of successfully coping with high-speed highways, complex traffic patterns, and from simply "growing up."

Driving a motor vehicle is an awesome responsibility, a privilege that must be earned, not a right. To earn that privilege you have to learn the rules and regulations the experts consider most important for all drivers to know, and observe them during every mile of your driving. That information is in this book.

MINOR'S PERMIT/PROVISIONAL LICENSE

Requirements for a Minor's Permit and a Provisional License are online at **www.dmv.ca.gov/pubs,** and in the DMV's *CALIFORNIA DRIVER HANDBOOK*. A *Teen Driver Guide* and a *Parent-Teen Driver Guide* are available online **www.dmv.ca.gov/pubs.**

Teen driver tests will contain the same questions as are in the practice tests in this book. Most of the questions are on the tests for Minor's Permits and Provisional Permits. If you are going to be out there driving with holders of Class C licenses, to drive legally and safely, you will need to know the same rules and regulations they do. Take DMVs online tests at: **www.dmv.ca.gov/pubs/interactive/drive/exam**
Read the statements on the following pages. Some of them may be answers to your test questions.

THINGS EVERY TEEN DRIVERS SHOULD KNOW

► The leading cause of deaths for teenagers is drunk driving.

► The most common violation for teen drivers is speeding.

► A common factor in the traffic deaths of new drivers is inexperience and lack of familiarity with their vehicle, and pushing themselves and their vehicle to the limit.

► Nearly <u>half</u> of all new drivers 15 to 19 are convicted of traffic violations during the first 12 months of their driving.

► Habitual truancy (skipping school) will cause the driving privilege of a minor age 13 or older to be delayed for one year.

► If you are under 18 years of age, your risk of a fatal accident is 2 ½ times that of the "average" driver.

► A Provisional Permit does <u>not</u> allow you to drive alone.

► A Provisional Permit is not valid until you start driving lessons with an instructor (at age 17 ½).

► New drivers should not become over confident in their driving ability or attempt risky driving maneuvers.

► Minors convicted of possessing a concealed weapon will have their license suspended or revoked.

► Your parents, or whoever assumes responsibility for your driving conduct can have your license canceled.

► If you drive after your parents have notified DMV to cancel your license, you are responsible for any damages you cause.

► A person under 21 years of age who drives with a blood alcohol content (BAC) of 0.01% is driving illegally.

► The person a minor practices driving with must be a licensed driver 25 years of age or older, and must be sitting in the front seat next to the driver.

► Teenagers have twice as many accidents as adult drivers, while driving only half as many miles.

► Minors convicted of possessing a concealable weapon, or live ammunition, will have their driving privilege suspended or revoked.

► A driver under 18 years of age may not talk on a cell phone while driving (Effective July 1, 2008) even if a hands-free device is used.

► Speeding accounts for about 50% of all teen traffic convictions

► A driver under 18 years of age may not send or listen to a text message while driving.

► If you drive with a Minor's Permit, a licensed driver 25 years of age or older must sit in the front seat with you, close enough to take hold of the wheel, should it become necessary.

PARENT-TEEN TEACHING HELP

Study **DMV's** *Parent-Teen Training Guide* before attempting to teach your teen to drive. It is available at DMV licensing offices and online.***www.dmv.gov/pubs***

If you teach your teen to drive you may have less patience with him or her than another family member or a friend. But you should try not to be overly critical. Point out his or her mistakes in a calm, helpful manner. Show them how to correct them.

Avoid ridicule or sarcasm. Your teen doesn't need to hear "Now why did you do that! If I told you once, I told you a thousand times...! Didn't I just tell you not to...? Will you never learn...?"

Keep in mind that your teen's mistakes are simply from a lack of experience and/or judgment. You can't expect him or her to learn in a few hours, or a few days, what you learned in many years of driving.

Professional driving lessons are expensive, but they are well worth the money in terms of wear and tear on the nerves of parents, and their teens. Dual-controls in the training car help the instructor remain calm. And they give the student a greater sense of security.

If your teen practices with you while taking professional driving lessons, don't tell him or her to do something different from the way their instructor taught them. It will confuse and frustrate them, and could cause them to fail their driving test.

> "A driver education course is the best insurance you can buy"

WARNINGS AND SUGGESTIONS, BEFORE YOU TAKE A BEHIND-THE-WHEEL TEST!

BAD DRIVING HABITS ARE HARD TO BREAK

If whoever taught you had any bad driving habits, they taught you those bad driving habits, and you may have since picked up some on your own.

A professional driving instructor will point them out to you and help you correct them. The instructor will show you everything you will have to do on your driving test, from the time you get in the car with the examiner, until the test is over. You may be allowed to practice on the actual DMV driving test route. If you are, you won't have the added stress of driving on unfamiliar streets.

Make a list of the things you see experienced drivers do that you think may be dangerous or illegal. If you are guilty of any of the things below, make a conscious effort to stop doing them.

Rolling through a stop sign, or just pausing briefly at a stop sign when no other cars are coming, is so much a habit of the majority of drivers, no matter how many times they say, "I wouldn't do it on a driving test"—they *will* do it on a driving test! You have made a legal stop only when your wheels have stopped rolling, and you have looked left, right, and left again for any nearby traffic.

Making a left turn in front of an oncoming vehicle so close it has to slow down to keep from hitting you *(Failure to yield right-of-way),* is an immediate test failure.

Swinging partially over into the next lane when making a right or left turn may cause you to fail. If a car had been in that lane you may have hit it *(Failure to stay in your lane)*. Sloppy turns are illegal, and can cause you to fail your test.

Driving off the pavement to pass a car, following another vehicle too closely (Tailgating), and **passing another car on a solid line** (even if the driver is as slow as Christmas), is illegal and dangerous.

During your driving test you must drive at all times as if there were a car on your left, on your right, behind you and ahead of you. The examiner will grade you that way.

PRACTICE! PRACTICE! PRACTICE!

Get lots of practice. I mean, hours and hours!

Don't spend all your practice time driving on long straight roads. An examiner kept telling a woman to make a right turn as they approached street after street. She kept driving straight ahead. Finally he ordered her to stop and let him drive her car back to the licensing office. When he asked her why she hadn't followed his orders, she said she had not learned to make turns, only to drive straight!

You'll do very little straight driving on a test. Practice making smooth right and left turns, backing up in a straight line, and making smooth, gentle stops.

Until you have learned the basics of safe driving, an excellent practice area is an area where houses are going to be built, where the streets are already laid out and paved. When you feel comfortable driving there, practice in quiet residential areas until you are ready to venture into heavier traffic.

THE BEHIND-THE-WHEEL DRIVING TEST

For most of us any kind of test is nerve-wracking. But if one is unprepared, a behind-the-wheel driving test can be downright traumatic. An instructor can teach you everything he or she knows about driving, but cannot calm your nerves when the examiner climbs into the car with you. The best and only way to combat nervousness is to practice, practice, practice.

Try to schedule an early morning appointment for your test. And as was said before, you should eat a good breakfast. Feed your brain.

Dress neatly. Green or purple hair may be acceptable, but it should be neat and clean. If you have piercings: in your nose, eyelids, lips, tongue or ears, remove some of their baubles and bangles. To those who wear droopy drawers, saggy pants or whatever you call them, pull them up over your backside. Tie your shoe laces. Some driver examiners are not much into "cool."

Experienced drivers are graded the same as new drivers, strictly by the book. If you are an older driver, don't expect to be graded differently than younger drivers. No allowances are made for age, nor does your age count against you.

All drivers, young and old, are graded on their knowledge of the laws, and their ability to handle an automobile safely.

BOOST THE EXAMINER'S CONFIDENCE

If you take professional driving lessons, you may also use the driving school's car to take your test in. Taking you test in a car with a brake and a steering wheel on the examiner's side of the car may help you make a better score. Knowing he or she can control the car helps the examiner observe your actions much more calmly.

if you use your own car for the test it must be properly insured, safe to drive, and one you are used to driving. It is easier to pass a test in a car with automatic transmission than in one with standard transmission.

EQUIPMENT CHECK / VEHICLE REGISTRATION

Your car's equipment must be in safe working order. Headlights, brake lights, taillights and tires must be in good condition. Electric turn signals must work well. Front windows must roll down. The Emergency/Parking brake must work. You will have to demonstrate that you know how to operate your vehicle's equipment, and that you know the proper hand and arm signals. You will not be asked to use hand and arm signals on the test if your electric signals are working, but you should know them. The hand and arm signals are in DMV's Driver Handbook, and in this book.

Make sure your current vehicle registration is in the glove compartment, your wallet or your purse. You will also have to show proof of financial responsibility (liability insurance) Page 46.

SOME NO-NO'S

Have your car clean. If you smoke, empty the ashtrays and air out the car. Clean the windshield and windows. No pets or passengers in the car. No coaching from bystanders. No alcohol on your breath. No smoking. No music. No thrumming your fingers on the dashboard. No pop cans rolling around on the floor. No left foot braking. No one-handed palming of the wheel. No steering with one finger; that makes the examiner want to rap your knuckles. And it really doesn't look cool. It looks and is dangerous! If you should hit an object or a chuckhole in the road, the steering wheel could be jerked out of your hands. Keep both hands on the wheel, the **9** and **3** positions.

THINGS TO DO WHILE BEING TESTED

These are some of the things you will be graded on when you take the behind the wheel test. Some of them are repeated and are explained in detail in other places in the book.

• **Adjust your seat** *before* **you fasten your safety belt.**

• **Adjust your mirrors** *after* **you adjust your seat.**

• **Don't grind the starter when you start the car. Release it the instant the engine starts.**

• **Don't forget to give the proper signal when entering traffic from the DMV parking lot.**

• **Keep your hands at the 9 and 3 positions on the steering wheel.**

• **Look in the mirrors and over your shoulders before changing lanes.**

• **Check your rearview mirror before stopping.**

• **Stop before the crosswalk or the limit line.**

• **Remove your foot from the accelerator when you brake, or you may get rattled and press the accelerator and brake at the same time. Or, you may press the accelerator when you need to press the brake.**

- Make right and left turns smoothly. Don't throw the examiner around in the car.

- Make your turns into the proper lanes: right turns close to the curb and into the right lane; left turns wide and squarely into the left lane.

- Keep your eye on other drivers at intersections. If one motions for you to take the right-of-way, take it. Don't sit there waving, "On no, be my guest!"

- Watch   for children or animals who may be about to run into the street.

- Give bicyclists a wide berth.

- Watch for cars pulling out of parking spaces; or backing out. Be ready to give them a friendly toot. Or stop and let them out.

- If   traffic is flowing freely enough, maintain a steady speed.

- If you have to drive on the freeway don't stop before entering it, unless it is absolutely necessary.

- Enter the freeway at about the same speed as freeway traffic is moving.

- Enter   the right lane and stay there, unless the examiner instructs you to change lanes.

- Adjust your speed to that of freeway traffic

- If you are instructed to cross several lanes of freeway traffic, signal before each lane change.

- Don't leave your lane to pass a car on the freeway unless you are instructed to.

- If you are behind a car that is just too slow, you may ask the examiner if you should pass it.

- Make sure you know the proper passing technique:

Signal. Look over your shoulder. Pull out. When you can see the car's headlights in your rearview mirror, give a right signal and pull back into the lane in front of it.

- Drive defensively. Check your mirrors before slowing down or stopping.

- Keep your eyes moving. Scan the roadway ahead, behind, and to the sides of your vehicle.

- Maintain a "space cushion" around your vehicle.

- Don't tailgate. Stay five car lengths behind the car in front of you. Try to anticipate the actions of other drivers. Be ready to take the proper evasive action.

- If you see something that might require evasive action on your part, tell the examiner: "I see that...."

- When you see the examiner's pen move don't worry about how he or she may be grading you. Keep your eyes on the road.

List other things you should not do on the test:

_____

_____

_____

_____

THE ROAD TEST

Take your cue from the examiner. Be friendly, but not too chatty unless he or she invites it. Treat the examiner with respect. "Yes Maam" and "Yes Sir" will not detract from your score.

It won't be necessary for you to open the passenger-side door and tuck a female examiner safely inside. She may be adept at climbing up into mile-high Humvees, and hopping over the closed doors of little sports cars and landing expertly on the seat. As this writer could—once upon a time!

As soon as you get in the car adjust your seat and mirrors and fasten your seat belt, to avoid fumbling with them after the examiner gets in. But before starting off, eye them critically. Touch the inside mirror as if you are making a minor adjustment. Peer at the outside mirrors. Let the examiner know *you* know these things should be done *before* starting the car.

Don't start the car until the examiner has explained what you can expect on the test. Pay close attention to her instructions. If you don't understand an instruction, don't guess at it. Ask the examiner to explain exactly what you are to do.

RELAX, LISTEN, STAY COOL

The examiner's job is to determine if you can operate a motor vehicle safely; to see how closely you follow the rules of the road and if you show the proper attitude toward other drivers. **No tricks will be played on you.**

You will be expected to obey every order, but with caution. Listen carefully to the examiner's instructions. Don't prattle on like a Nervous Nellie. The examiner may **decide you are too shaky to take the test.**

When the examiner has finished instructing you, start the car smoothly. Don't grind the ignition. Don't start off too fast. Look all around your car before moving, and signal if necessary. **If you have been allowed to practice on the actual DMV road test, and know that the next thing you will probably do is make a right or left turn, don't go ahead and put on a turn signal.**

The examiner may fail you for not following her orders. You will be told what to do in time to signal, get in the proper lane, prepare for a turn, slow down, or stop.

NO PEEKING

The examiner's pen will be going "Check! Check! Check!" on her clipboard. Don't be alarmed, she may be checking "Good. Good. Good." Furtive little glances to see how you are being graded may cause you to miss something. Keep your eyes on the road.

SIGNAL. CHECK YOUR MIRRORS. LOOK OVER YOUR SHOULDERS.

Don't forget to signal, even when there are no cars around. Check traffic in your mirrors and over your shoulders before you change lanes, make a turn, or stop. Check your mirrors often. All of them: the rearview mirror and both outside mirrors.

You don't need to act like a bobble-head doll, but you should make sure the examiner knows when you look over your shoulders, even if you have to exaggerate a bit. Swivel your head further around. Don't just glance left, right, and left, with tiny little movements of your head, or a quick flick of the eyeballs. Turn your head this way and that.

This writer remembers taking a behind-the-wheel test in Los Angeles many years ago, and being complimented by the examiner for looking over her left shoulder before making a left turn. She said "Thanks, but doesn't everyone?" He said: "Not hardly!"

Keep your hands at the 9 and 3 positions on the steering wheel. For many years the 10 and 2 positions were recommended. Experts now say the 9 and the 3 positions are safer, because if the airbag should deploy there is less chance of an injury to your hands and arms.

AT INTERSECTIONS

When approaching an intersection, even if the light has just changed to green, be ready to brake. A vehicle approaching from the left or right may speed up when their light changes to yellow and sail on through on the red light. If the light has been green for a while, be ready to brake. It may be about to change to red. If you are told to make a turn just past the intersection, don't put on a turn signal until you are *in* the intersection. If you do, another driver may think you are going to turn right or left into the intersection and pull out in front of you when you continue on through.

In city traffic, look ahead of your vehicle a full block. Glance left, and right, near and far. Knowing what is ahead of you, behind you and to the sides of your vehicle, "scanning", will help you avoid having to stop quickly or make unsafe lane changes.

When you see a vehicle approaching your road from a side road, go ahead and place your foot on the brake. If you say quietly, "I see 'em," the examiner will not think that you are an overly cautious driver, but one who is always ready for what may be about to happen. (See **DMVs Driver Handbook** for more information about intersections).

FREEWAY DRIVING?

Find out if your test will include freeway driving. To have to enter a freeway soon after your test starts can be frightening, but the examiner will tell you in plenty of time for you to locate the on-ramp and make your entrance safely.

You will enter the freeway at an on-ramp and merge into the right lane and stay there, unless the examiner tells you to change lanes.

If you have not had much freeway driving experience, practice entering and exiting the freeway near the DMV testing area.

RIGHT AND LEFT TURNS

When making right and left turns, stay in your lane. Drive at all times as if there were a car in the lane next to the one you are turning into. Make right turns close to the curb but don't bump it.

To prevent cutting left turns too close, wait until the front bumper of your car gets to the edge of the lane you are turning into before turning your wheels. Turn sharply. When your car is headed squarely into your lane, straighten your wheels quickly and resume your speed.

STRAIGHT LINE BACKING

You must be able to back your car in a straight line for about 50 feet. You must not back over into the lane beside you, not even a few inches over the dividing line. Back slowly so you can make corrections if you start to go off course. The examiner may suggest a speed at which you should back up. If he doesn't tell you how fast to go, you should back at a speed of about 15 miles an hour.

Backing up is safer and easier with a back-up mirror, but if your car doesn't have one, follow the steps below:

When you are told to start backing, change to **REVERSE.** Look in front of your car and over your left shoulder, to see if a car is in the left lane. If one is there, don't start backing until it has passed you. Put your left hand at the top of the steering wheel at **12 o'clock high**. Turn your body to the right until you have a full view of the back of your car and both sides of the street. Place your right arm on the top of the passenger seat.

To back in a straight line, you barely touch your steering wheel right and left, so easy the wheel hardly moves. New drivers with very little backing practice may have difficulty "thinking in reverse." They may momentarily forget how to make the car go where they want it to go when in REVERSE.

Going backward is exactly like going forward, if you want the rear end to go to the right, turn (touch) the steering wheel to the right. If you want the rear end to go to the left, turn (touch) the wheel to the left.

Back slowly, *but don't creep.* If you start going out of your lane, across the center line, or too near the side of the road, STOP! Get your bearings and start again. Backing into a curb, or into the other lane, will cause you to fail. Check to the front and sides. a time or two (quick glances) while you are backing. When the examiner tells you to stop, brake gently and stop smoothly. If he is looking back with you as you are backing, when he tells you to stop he may turn quickly and look to the front. Your natural reaction will probably be to turn around when he does, but don't do it. He is testing you to see how you would react to your passenger's actions. How easily you are distracted.

But why should you keep looking back until your wheels stop rolling? Because a little child or a pet can be under your back wheels in an *instant.* When your car has stopped rolling, change to **DRIVE** and drive forward.

Down the road a bit you may be told to turn your car around in the street, without hitting the curb, or driving off the pavement, and go back the way you came. (Oh no! How do I do that?) You can. Read on.

THREE-POINT TURN

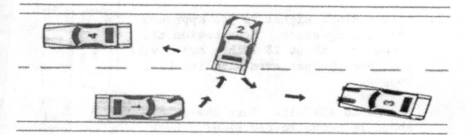

1.Give a RIGHT signal, stop as close to the right curb as possible without touching it. Give a LEFT signal. Turn your wheels sharp left **(Car #1)**. Check traffic ahead and behind. Drive across the street. Don't bump the curb. Change to REVERSE. Turn your wheels sharp RIGHT **(Car #2)**.

2. Check traffic both ways. Look back over your right shoulder and back across the street **(Car # 3)**. No signal necessary before backing.

3. Change to DRIVE. Straighten your wheels. Check traffic. Drive forward in the proper lane **(Car #4)**. No signal necessary.

Practice the 3-Point Turn until you can do it without bumping the curb or driving off the pavement.

The purpose of the 3-Point Turn is to see how well you can handle your vehicle in a tight spot.

PARALLEL PARKING

1. Give a RIGHT signal as you approach
   the parking space. Stop beside the
   front car, about 18 inches away, with
   your back bumper even with its back
   bumper.

   Change to REVERSE. Turn the wheel
   about 1½ turns to the RIGHT. Back
   slowly, easing the wheel another ½
   turn to the RIGHT, until the corner
   of your windshield is opposite the
   bumper of the front car, and your
   left rear fender points to the center
   of the rear car.

2. Turn wheel about 2 full turns LEFT.
   Watch the front of your car so it
   doesn't touch the other car, and
   back slowly until your rear bumper
   almost touches the rear car.

3. Change to DRIVE. Turn wheel 2 turns
   RIGHT. Creep forward. Straighten
   wheels as you move. Straighten
   evenly between the two cars. You
   should be between 12 and 18 inches
   from the curb.

> Instructions are for parking average
> size vehicle, about 8 X 18 feet.
> Larger or smaller vehicles, adjust
> number turns of steering wheel.

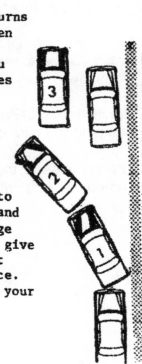

TO EXIT THE PARKING SPACE change to
REVERSE, turn wheels SHARP RIGHT and
back close to the rear car. Change
to DRIVE, turn wheels SHARP LEFT, give
a LEFT signal, look over your left
shoulder and drive out of the space.
Straighten the wheels and stay in your
lane as you drive forward.

112

IT'S OVER !

When the test is over and you are safely back in the DMV parking lot, turn off your engine, hold your knees together so they don't knock, and wait (patiently) until the examiner has finished grading your test. He will go over it with you and tell you the mistakes you made, the things you did well, and if you passed. If you didn't pass, or barely scraped by, check violations below. The reason is probably there.

• <u>Rolling</u> **through a stop sign. (Number One reason for test failure).**
• **Stopping too quickly or stopping quickly without checking your rearview mirrors.**
• **Swinging too wide (into the wrong lane) on your turns or cutting them too close. (You hit a car in the other lane!)**
• **The examiner had to grab the steering wheel, or give you an instruction to prevent an accident**
• **Failure to follow the examiner's orders.**
• **Failure to yield right-of-way**
• **Hitting or bumping a curb**
• **Driving off the road or street**
• **Driving too slowly**
• **And the biggest "No- No"--speeding.**

If you passed, keep that great smile on your face until the Photo Shoot is over (Page 93). Then, for the rest of your life, drive as carefully as you did on your test.

SAFER DRIVING FOR SENIORS

Older drivers are more often held at fault when they are involved in a traffic situation where violations occur. They are charged with failing to yield right of way, improper left turns and lane changes, failing to observe stop signs and signals, pulling out in front of other drivers dangerously, and driving too slow on busy highways. Inattention to these driving tasks and lack of concentration are the primary reasons for their driving problems.

HOW TO KEEP YOUR DRIVER LICENSE

You can delay, and possibly prevent ever having to give up your driver license. Taking **AARP's** *MATURE DRIVER IMPROVEMENT COURSE* will greatly reduce the risk of you causing an accident and injuring someone. It will bring you up to date on new traffic laws and road rules, and will heighten your awareness of the dangers of *not* following them every mile of your driving. Taking the course may also qualify you for an insurance premium discount.

Your local Council on Aging can tell you when and where the course is held. Or you may find it online at **www.aarp.org**.

And of course this writer always recommends professional driving instructions to sharpen your driving skills.

The suggestions on the following pages may be helpful if you find that you are having more near misses on the road; you get lost; other drivers honk at you often; you have been involved in a collision, or have difficulty reading ordinary signs. If you are beginning to feel apprehensive about your driving, more hesitant to get behind the wheel, the course will restore some of your confidence.

• Always ask your doctor about the side effects of any prescribed medications.

• Stay alert at the wheel. Concentrate on your driving. Don't let your mind wander. Don't day dream. Don't plan the evening meal while driving. Don't rehearse the speech you are planning to give at your club. Don't talk on a cell phone. Don't text. Don't leave the radio on. Don't let your attention linger on distractions outside, or inside your car. Before you know it a vehicle can slow down or stop in front of you

• Don't drive with children in the car. They can distract you.

• If you have difficulty seeing all around your car, sit on a cushion. Make sure your vehicle is equipped with power steering, power brakes, larger mirrors, and automatic seat adjustment. If you find that when you start off your car lurches forward, lower your foot on the accelerator, press the accelerator with the ball of your foot. Keep your heel on the floor. Driving shoes are expensive, but may well be worth the price because of the comfort and safety they provide.

• Every few seconds while driving remind yourself to: "Look to the sides, and back to the road ahead (quickly)! Look in the mirrors and back to the road ahead (quickly)! Look over your shoulder and back to the road ahead (quickly)!"

• Play the "What If Game." Try to anticipate any unsafe actions of other drivers. Ask yourself what you would do if a driver in a parked car suddenly pulled out in front of you, or backed out of a parking space on the side of the street. What if you see two legs pushing open the door of a parked car? Can you stop, or is there a car on your bumper? Can you swerve into the next lane? What if a bicycle in the next lane should suddenly turn in front of you, or fall in front of you? Can you stop? Are there children playing near the street? A ball is rolling into the street; cover your brake. A rolling ball usually has a child behind it. If an animal darts into the street, stop if you can do so safely. But don't endanger your life for that of an animal.

• Brake lights and turn signals, and wheels turning toward the street are warning signals. If you are driving beside another car, glance at its front wheels. Are they easing toward your lane, about to cut in front of you? Are you in a driver's blind spot? Drop back or move ahead of the car. You are driving up a hill, what is on the other side? A line of cars stopped just over the crest of the hill at a traffic light? A stalled car? An accident?

• Avoid backing whenever possible. Park where you can exit the parking place by driving forward. Before backing out of a parking space move your car a few inches. Are your wheels straight, or turned right or left? Make sure they are straight before you move any further, or bam! you'll hit a car parked next to you.

• Stay closer to the center line of the street when passing bicyclists in your lane
• Don't drive on freeways or in any congested fast-moving traffic, except when necessary.
• Stay at least 3 seconds behind the driver in front of you.
• Try to figure out what other drivers may be about to do. What will you do if they present a danger to you?

Keep your eyes moving. Leave yourself an "out."

BACK SEAT DRIVERS (Grr-r-r-rr!)

Don't allow yourself to become frustrated or angry by your passengers' well-meaning but annoying comments. Passengers can be good navigators, but don't depend entirely upon their advice as to when you should stop, pull out into traffic, or pass another car. Decide for yourself if you can perform the maneuver safely. If your passenger insists upon criticizing your driving and telling you every move to make, stop the car, get out, and don't get back in until he or she agrees to dummy up.

AVOID THE RUSH HOURS

Plan your local trips between the rush hours of 10 A.M. and 3 P.M.

MORE SAFETY TIPS FOR OLDER DRIVERS

- **Stay physically active**
- **Schedule regular vision and hearing tests**
- **Manage any chronic conditions**
- **Understand your limitations**
- **Plan ahead**
- **Drive only when you feel up to it**
- **Let someone know where you are going and when you expect to be back**
- **Update your driving skills**

Get a copy of DMVs *SENIOR GUIDE FOR SAFE DRIVING.* Online at **www.dmv.gov** or pick up one at a DMV Licensing Office near you.

NIGHT DRIVING AND VISION

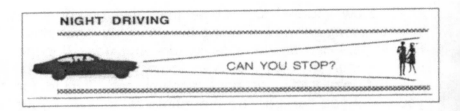

IF YOU MUST DRIVE AT NIGHT

Choose well-marked, well-lighted streets with easy to read signs and easily accessible parking. Don't overdrive your headlights. Make sure you can stop in the distance your lights shine ahead of your car. Drive at a reduced speed and stay in the right lane as much as possible. Avoid driving in the rain at night. Rain causes glare from headlights and makes it hard to see pavement markings.

REDUCED VISION

At night, the 20/20 vision of most people is reduced to about 20/50. Through a dirty windshield, or on a rainy night, cataracts, traffic lights, brake lights and street lights and headlights, may be a confusion of shimmering colors, blotting out forms, vehicles, pedestrians, signs and pavement markings.

GLARE RECOVERY

The field of glare from approaching headlights may be larger than the vehicle itself. A 55 year-old driver takes eight times as long to recover from glare as a 16-year-old. At 55 miles per hour, a car travels about 80 feet per second. An older person will drive 640 feet virtually blind before his or her eyes recover from the glare.

SIDE VISION or PERIPHERAL VISION

Peripheral vision, the distance you can see to the right and left "out of the corners of your eyes," narrows with age. You may be able to see what is on the right side of the road, while the left side may be a blur or continuous dark shadow. Depth perception decreases, affecting your ability to tell how close or how far you are from a car or an object ahead. Drive in the right lane as much as possible. Turn your head often. Take quick looks. But only a quick look! Your eyes off the road for more than an instant can be too long. Your car can leave the road before you know it.

DRIVING IN FADING LIGHT

More accidents happen at dusk than any other time of the day. Be careful about passing at dusk. A car coming toward you may not have its lights on. Use electric turn signals at night. Hand and arm signals cannot be seen. Never wear sunglasses at night.

DRIVING TEST MAY BE REQUIRED

If you are involved in two or more accidents in a year, if your eyesight is 20/200 or worse, or if anyone has reported to DMV that you should be re-examined for any reason, you may have to take another written test and a behind- the-wheel driving test.

If your doctor or anyone else notifies DMV that perhaps you should stop driving, you will be called in for reexamination. Don't panic. You may have let some bad habits creep into your driving that a professional refresher course can take care of. Or you may simply need new eyeglasses.

TIPS FOR ALL DRIVERS

HEADLIGHTS

When you are within 500 feet of a vehicle coming toward you, dim your headlights by switching to low beams. You may need to flash your lights to remind a driver coming toward you to dim his or her lights. That means a flash of **no more than an instant.** Make sure they are far enough away that the flash doesn't blind them.

Don't look directly at oncoming cars. Look toward the right edge of your lane until they have passed. If you try to "get even" with the other driver by leaving your high beams on, there will be two blind drivers bearing down on each other.

When you are following another vehicle at night, and you get within 300 feet of it, switch to low beams. High beams will hit the rearview mirror of the vehicle ahead and blind the driver. If you are being followed closely, turn your mirror to the night driving position.

WARN OTHER DRIVERS

Before turning into a street or a driveway, or stopping, check your rearview mirror for vehicles following closely. If one appears to be too close and the driver is staring off into space, looking off to the side of the road, or talking on a cell phone, tap your brake lights several times until the driver notices them and backs off. Watch for the space between your car and the one behind to expand. If that doesn't happen, the car may hit you as you slow down to turn. Keep driving until you can make a turn safely.

USE YOUR HORN *ONLY* WHEN NECESSARY

There are horn beepers, and there are horn blasters. A friendly beep with a smile, a slight nod, or a little wave, is usually appreciated. A blast may anger, rattle or infuriate another driver. It may also cause a motorist with a cell phone to call a California Highway Patrol (CHP) and suggest that he or she drive behind you a few miles and try to figure out what your problem is: a bad hair day, alcohol or drugs, road rage, or something else. Use your horn only when necessary to prevent an accident.

LIGHTS, WIPERS AND DEFROSTER CONTROLS

If you don't do much night driving or driving in the rain, you may not be able to operate your light controls, wipers or defrosters without fumbling. Practice in your driveway until you can operate them without taking your eyes off the road. There is nothing more frightening than to be caught in a sudden rain storm or have another vehicle cover your windshield with a huge splash of water, and you can't find your wipers.

DON'T DRIVE YOURSELF TO DISTRACTION

- Be cooperative and polite on the road.
- Don't scream or yell at another driver, or make obscene gestures.
- Don't blast the horn at someone daydreaming at a traffic light. Tap the horn gently.
- Obey the speed limit, don't weave from lane to lane.
- Avoid eye contact with an angry driver.
- When someone antagonizes you, don't fight back. Take a deep breath and breathe a little prayer that his or her bad manners won't result in a tragic accident.

- At a slow traffic light, don't sit there with your stomach tied in a knot. Take some deep breaths. Breathe in ... breathe out ... breathe in ... breathe out. The light will change before you know it.

- **Tell yourself, "I'll get there when I get there!"**

SECURITY ON THE ROAD FOR ALL DRIVERS.

Have your vehicle serviced before starting out. Carry a flashlight, emergency flasher or some type of warning system in case it breaks down. If a tire goes flat or your vehicle starts acting strangely, put on your hazard lights. They will work even with the ignition off. Ease your foot off the accelerator, brake gently, signal your intentions and try to work your way to the side of the road or a breakdown lane.

Once off the road, raise your hood. If you have any warning signs set them 200-300 feet to the rear of your vehicle. On a two-way traffic road set them 200-300 feet in front of your vehicle.

LET SOMEONE KNOW YOU NEED HELP

If you can't fix the problem, get back in your car and lock the doors. If you have a cell phone, call 911 for assistance. At night, turn on your dome light.

If someone stops and offers to help you, ask them to call CHP if you haven't already done so. If they don't leave and are making you uneasy, continue to sit in your car with windows and doors locked until reliable help arrives.

Do not open your door to strangers, day or night, unless you are sure you are in a safe place. Don't accept a stranger's offer to take you home, or some place to get help. You may *never* get there!

REST AREAS

Be very careful when stopping at rest areas where no security is provided. Don't stop at an unguarded rest area at night unless several other cars are there. If you leave your car, lock your purse, cameras and other valuables in the trunk. Lock the doors. If you take a nap at a rest area, lock the doors and roll up the windows.

If someone tries to get in your car or assault or rob you, honk the horn, flash your lights, push the panic button on your car key fob to attract the attention of someone who may come to your rescue. The intruder may flee. **Do not allow young children to go to the restrooms alone.**

OTHER USES FOR THE PANIC BUTTON

If you can't find your car in a parking lot, push the panic button on your car key fob. If you are near enough, your car will honk and flash its parking lights at you. In a parking garage your panic button may be helpful in locating your car.

Put your car keys on your bedside table at night. If someone is trying to break in, push the panic button. It should scare them away.

To silence the car alarm, press the panic button for a few seconds.

SHOULD YOU STOP AT NIGHT TO HELP A STRANDED MOTORIST?

If you have a cell phone call CHP. Or stop at a call box and ask for assistance for the stranded motorist. Tell them you will wait nearby until help arrives. If they insist they don't need you, leave. If you stay, they may be afraid you are not the Good Samaritan you appear to be.

IF YOU ARE REAR-ENDED

If you are rear-ended at night in an unsafe place, keep going. Drive to a police station or call the police. If you stop and get out of your car you may be robbed, attacked or kidnapped.

A reminder: If you are involved in an accident, even if you suspect the accident may have been your fault, do not apologize. Show your concern, attend the injured as well as you can, but wait for an investigation before deciding who should apologize.

EXCHANGE INFORMATION

Exchange information with the other driver: name, address, driver license number, vehicle registration and the name of your insurance company. But don't discuss amounts of coverage. Mention of large amounts may cause exaggerated damage and injury reports. Don't talk about what you *think* happened. Don't argue with the other driver. Try to get names and addresses of any witnesses. Ask what they saw. If the other driver refuses to cooperate, record his or her license plate number and the make and model of the car. They can be subpoenaed as witnesses. Don't leave the scene of an accident unless the other driver becomes abusive. If that happens, you should drive to the nearest police station. Notify your insurance company as soon as possible.

WHEN IN DOUBT, CHECK 'EM OUT

If it is broad daylight and you are being chased on a busy highway by a vehicle with lights flashing and sirens screaming, you can probably assume a real police officer is after you. But if you are on a lonely road and have no idea what you have done wrong, and the vehicle chasing you is not well marked, keep going. If you are forced to stop, don't turn off the ignition. Open the window a tiny bit. Ask them to hold their ID up to the window. If they show you a weapon, burn rubber. Keep driving until you come to a well-lighted area. Call 911.

LAW ENFORCEMENT STOP

When you are stopped by someone you are sure is a real police officer, turn on your right signal and drive to the right side of the road or freeway. Don't stop in a driving lane, a freeway median or on the left side of a two-way roadway. On a freeway, move completely onto the right shoulder. Turn off your radio. End your cell phone chat, if any. If your windows are heavily tinted, roll your window down. Don't start fumbling for your driver license. Place both hands at the top of the steering wheel. Tell your passengers to keep their hands on their laps. Don't get out of your car unless the officer asks you to. Never reach over to take your wallet or vehicle registration from the glove compartment without asking the officer if you may do so. You could be staring down a gun barrel when you raise up. Police officers can't be too careful either!

Dear Library Patron:

Please do not remove this page from the book. Copy the information on your library's copy machine. Make extra copies for friends.

ORDER FORM:

I would like to order _____copy (copies) of
CALIFORNIA DRIVERS TEST MADE EASY @ 13.99 each.
I have added $3.00 for shipping & handling. Enclosed is a

Check ☐   Money order for ☐ **$**_____

Please print:

Name _____

Street/Apt. # _____

City _____

State _____ ZIP _____

Phone: _____

email:_____(optional)

Send payment to:
Syman Publishing
P.O. Box 5495
St. Augustine, FL 32085
Contact us: 904-810-5596
asyman@earthlink.net